THE FAITH

Dedication

To
B.E.C.
my Mother
my Best Friend

THE FAITH SERIES

The Faith
Understanding Orthodox Christianity

The Way
*What Every Protestant Should Know
about the Orthodox Church*

The Truth
*What Every Roman Catholic Should Know
about the Orthodox Church*

The Life
The Orthodox Doctrine of Salvation

Available from Regina Orthodox Press,
www.reginaorthodoxpress.com, Toll Free 800-636-2470

THE FAITH

Understanding Orthodox Christianity

An Orthodox Catechism

Clark Carlton

Editorial Committee

Archbishop DMITRI of Dallas
Bishop ISAIAH of Denver
Bishop BASIL of Wichita
Archimandrite Peter

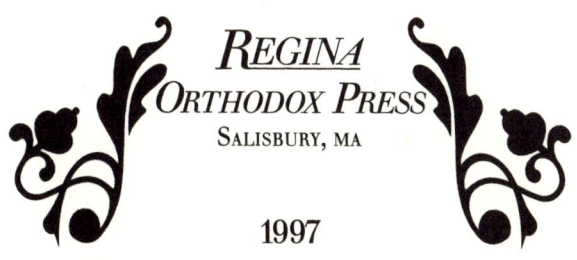

REGINA
ORTHODOX PRESS
SALISBURY, MA

1997

© Clark Carlton, 1997

ISBN 978-0-9649141-1-7

Cover Photo: Colombe Che Bevono. Tomb of Galla Placidia; Ravenna, Italy. Used by permission.

All Scripture quotations are from the King James Version unless otherwise noted. Some quotations have been amended by the author to better reflect the original Greek text.

Regina Orthodox Press
P.O. Box 5288
Salisbury, MA 01952
1-800-636-2470
FAX: 978-462-5079

Contents

About the Author	8
Forewords	9
Archbishop DMITRI	
Bishop ISAIAH	
Bishop BASIL	
Archimandrite Peter	
Preface	17
Introduction	19
What is the Orthodox Church?	
The Symbol of Faith	38

Part One
The Doctrines of Christ

Chapter One	41
The Foundation of the Orthodox Faith	
Special Study: The Sign of the Cross	
Chapter Two	53
The Holy Trinity	
Special Study: The Trinity in the Old Testament	
Chapter Three	65
Creation	
Special Study: Creation and Evolution	
Chapter Four	79
The Fall of Mankind	
Special Study: The Passions	

CONTENTS

CHAPTER FIVE — 91
    The Promised Messiah of Israel
    Special Study: Typology

CHAPTER SIX — 103
    The Incarnation
    Special Study: Icon of the Invisible God

CHAPTER SEVEN — 115
    Man's "Yes" to God
    Special Study: Fervent Intercessors

CHAPTER EIGHT — 127
    The Teachings of Christ
    Special Study: Saving Humility

CHAPTER NINE — 139
    Love Stronger than Death
    Special Study: Great and Holy Saturday

Part Two
The Life In Christ

CHAPTER TEN — 153
    The Birth and Mission of the Church
    Special Study: Missions and Evangelism

CHAPTER ELEVEN — 165
    The Structure of the Church
    Special Study: Ecumenical Councils

CHAPTER TWELVE — 179
    Holy Baptism
    Special Study: The Baptism of Tears

CONTENTS

CHAPTER THIRTEEN — 191
The Seal of the Gift of the Holy Spirit
Special Study: The Fruits of the Spirit

CHAPTER FOURTEEN — 203
The Mystical Supper
Special Study: The Communion of Saints

CHAPTER FIFTEEN — 215
The Church at Prayer
Special Study: Fasting

CHAPTER SIXTEEN — 227
The Mystery of Love
Special Study: God and Gender

CHAPTER SEVENTEEN — 239
Monasticism
Special Study: The Holy Mountain

CHAPTER EIGHTEEN — 251
The Lord's Return
Special Study: Heaven and Hell

CONCLUSION — 263
Living an Orthodox Life in a
Secular World

RECOMMENDED READING — 278

About the Author

Clark Carlton was born in Cookeville, Tennessee in 1964 and reared as a Southern Baptist. He earned a B.A. in philosophy from Carson-Newman College in Jefferson City, Tennessee. While studying as a Raymond Bryan Brown Memorial Scholar at the Southeastern Baptist Theological Seminary in Wake Forest, North Carolina, he converted to the Orthodox Faith and was chrismated at the St. Gregory the Great Orthodox Mission in Raleigh. The story of his conversion, "From First Baptist to the First Century," was published in *The Christian Activist* (Volume 10, 1997).

Mr. Carlton earned a Master of Divinity degree from St. Vladimir's Orthodox Theological Seminary in Crestwood, New York in 1990. His senior thesis, under the direction of Fr. John Meyendorff, was entitled "The Humanity of Christ According to St. Maximus the Confessor."

In 1993, he earned an M.A. in Early Christian Studies from the Catholic University of America in Washington, D.C. At present he is working as an adjunct instructor of philosophy at Tennessee Technological University in his home town while completing his Ph.D. dissertation on the dogmatic and ascetical theology of St. Mark the Monk (5th c.).

Forewords

Archbishop DMITRI

In his essay, "The Lost Scriptural Mind," Father Georges Florovsky, perhaps the twentieth century's most notable theologian, decries the "neglect of theology in the instruction given to the laity in modern times." He is not fantasizing when he says that "both clergy and laity are hungry for theology."

Clark Carlton's *The Faith: Understanding Orthodox Christianity* is a theological work. It is of the kind that can contribute greatly to satisfying the hunger of which Father Florovsky speaks. On the other hand, it is no dry catalog of doctrines and dogmas. Every part of the book is expressed in a lively and absorbing manner. In my mind, one of its most important features is the way in which the author makes the presentation of each doctrine or dogma a call to the life in Christ. The purpose or aim that shines through on every page is the salvation of our souls.

Mr. Carlton's deep understanding of the meaning of key scriptural passages, as well as the support for his explanations that he draws from the Fathers, both ancient and modern, make this work an indispensable guide for Orthodox Christians who want to know their faith and for those who are in search of authentic Christianity. His facing crucial issues of our times, in the text itself, in the questions posed in the "Reflections," and especially in the "Conclusion," make the

FOREWORDS

whole presentation very contemporary. At the same time, his theology is very traditional.

I pray that the Lord, the Father, the Son, and the Holy Spirit, may bless the author and his work for His glory and the building up of His holy Church.

⊹DMITRI
Archbishop of Dallas

* * *

Bishop ISAIAH

Many catechisms have been written by clergy and laity during the past fifty years, which for their time proved helpful to the reader, as well as edifying.

However, *The Faith* is by far the most orthodox in that it begins with the essential and basic premise of who God is. Without first identifying God as He has revealed Himself to us and building on this foundation, one can have a catechism that is simply a collection of questions and answers without necessarily allowing the reader to integrate the information and logically apply it to his personal life. Such a catechism of questions and answers creates the danger, moreover, of the reader interpreting those answers as man's responses, rather than God instructing us as to how we should believe and how we should worship Him.

It is not so with this catechism. This book is truly a *catechesis* in that it greatly assists the reader to know what and how an Orthodox Christian should believe, so that he may live in the world but not conform to the world. This catechism, then, is indeed superior to other previous attempts in teaching the true Faith, which is the only way to eternal life.

The format is akin to the Nicene-Constantinopolitan Creed in that God, the Father, the Son, and the Holy Spirit, is first presented according to the life of the Church which we call Holy Tradition, as well as Holy Scripture. In addition, a good number of the holy Fathers of the Church are quoted throughout the book, which enriches the book's contents in all of its subject matter.

The creation and the fall of mankind are then set before the reader in historic and chronological perspective, followed by the coming of Jesus Christ into the world as the prophesied Messiah. His teachings are then presented based on God's love for the world.

The mission and the structure of the Church are carefully explained on the basis of the Supreme Sacrifice of the Lord on the Cross. The sacraments of Baptism, Chrismation, and Confession are treated, not legalistically, but pastorally, thereby allowing the reader to identify himself as an active participant in these holy mysteries.

The chapter on the Mystical Supper is a powerful development—and correctly so—of the awesomeness of Holy Communion, awakening the reader to the fact that no one can receive the holy Body and Blood of Christ flippantly or even lightly. The chapters on marriage and celibacy are presented in a guileless manner, elevating both conditions in harmony with God's gifts to His people for their salvation.

FOREWORDS

Finally, the chapters on heaven and hell and God's unfading love throughout His creation allow the reader to return to the reality of the secular and, for the most part, atheistic world, not only enlightened and edified, but with a clear purpose as to his responsibilities regarding this world. He can better see how secularism and our consumeristic society minimizes and even negates the magnificence of God's creation from His crowning creature, man, to every blade of grass that sprouts forth out of the earth.

Although this catechism should be in the hands of every Orthodox Christian, regardless of nationality or racial and cultural heritage, it is the best-written catechism thus far for any person who wishes to understand the Faith and its theology in a very clear and comprehensive way from the truths in the Book of Genesis to the divinization of creation in the Book of Revelation.

Thus, it is obvious to one reading this work that God is and always has been consistent and true to His promises of a new heaven and a new earth in an unbroken sequence of historical events from the days of Adam and Eve, to the present, latter days, and on into eternity.

✣ISAIAH
Bishop of Denver

* * *

FOREWORDS

Bishop Basil

In our Church, neither patriarchs nor councils could ever introduce any novelty, because the protector of the faith among us is the very body of the Church, that is, our people themselves, who always desire to preserve their faith unchanged and in agreement with the faith of the Fathers.

This passage from the famous ENCYCLICAL LETTER TO ALL ORTHODOX CHRISTIANS, penned nearly a century and a half ago by Oecumenical Patriarch Anthimos VI and signed by the other Patriarchs of the East, clearly and succinctly sets forth a fundamental teaching of the Church: that the body of believers—clergy and laity together—is the guardian of divine truth. While it is true that the bishop is graced with the charisma of being teacher of the faith, it is also true that the protector, preserver and guardian of that faith *which was once for all delivered to the saints* (Jude 3) is not the episcopate alone, but the entire Body of Christ. Having understood this basic teaching, it should be perfectly clear why the publication of this present offering by Regina Orthodox Press is such a joyous—and vital—event in the life of the Church.

How does one protect, preserve and guard that which one does not know? How may falsehood be discerned if truth be not known? *The Faith: Understanding Orthodox Christianity*, a straightforward exposition of the faith written in a comfortable and easy-to-understand style, is precisely that which can help instruct believers in the doctrines and tenets of the faith, thus equipping them as with armor, which is the knowledge of truth. And truth, being neither merely theory nor philosophy but the very *theanthropos* Jesus Christ, is nothing less than Life itself. Serge S. Verhovskoy, the late and highly revered professor of dogmatic theology at St. Vladimir's Seminary, taught that the knowledge of truth coincides with the spiritual life; while ignorance, and even more than that, false knowledge, is spiritual death (*The Light of the World*, SVS Press: 1982, p. 11). *For we are not contending against flesh and blood*, as the holy Apostle Paul warns us, *but against principalities, against the powers, against the world rulers of this present darkness, against the spiritual hosts of wickedness in the heavenly places. Therefore take the whole armor of God, that you may be able to withstand in the evil day, and having done all, to stand* (Ephesians 6:12-13, Revised Standard Version).

The Faith is written, and useful, to two distinct audiences: those, as yet outside the one, holy, catholic and apostolic Church, but who are inquiring into or being catechized in the faith, and those who, already possessing the faith—or rather, being possessed by it—are responsible for its protection and preservation and to whom the ENCYCLICAL was and is addressed:

> the whole Orthodox society of the faithful, to the clergy and to the God-loving people, to the superiors and to the subordinates, to the rich and to the poor, to the parents and to the children, to the teachers and to the students, to the educated and to the ignorant.

FOREWORDS

May this book bring glory to the holy, consubstantial, life-giving and undivided Trinity, and contribute to the upbuilding of the holy Church and the salvation of souls.

✠BASIL
Titular Bishop of Enfeh
al-Koura
Wichita, Kansas

* * *

Archimandrite Peter

The One, Holy, Catholic and Apostolic Church of Christ—The Orthodox Church—is the *pillar and ground of the truth* (1 Timothy 3:15). This Truth is—immutable. It is found in both the Holy Scripture and the Holy Tradition, which the Church painstakingly, often times with great sacrifices to Herself, preserved without distortions, perversions or corruptions from the day She was founded on Pentecost, when the Holy Spirit descended on the Apostles.

Consequently, there can be nothing *new* in the Church. The truths that She teaches today in the modern world are exactly what She taught nineteen hundred years ago, at the dawn of Christianity. What She taught a thousand years ago among the Slavs, is precisely what She teaches today in Africa, or anywhere else.

What often changes is the approach.

FOREWORDS

The merit of this book is that the author is able to present eternal truths in a way that is comprehensible to modern man, in a way that he understands and can relate to.

When studying this book, one must also bear in mind that Orthodox dogma has moral significance. Saint Nikolai (Velimirovic) of the Serbian Orthodox Church writes: "If the dogma of faith seems at times to you to be tough food, you must first try to fulfill Christian moral dogma, and then the understanding of the dogma of faith will be revealed to you" (*The Prologue from Ochrid*, Part One, p. 59).

☦Archimandrite Peter
Holy Trinity Monastery
Jordanville, New York

Preface

The idea for this catechism was born in the early 1990's out of the need for a good, single-volume introduction to the Orthodox Faith. Being a convert myself, I was acutely aware of the needs of English-speaking seekers. In addition, having taught both youth and adult Sunday School classes, I was also aware of the general lack of theological knowledge among parishioners.

One of the major problems in regard to currently available literature is what has been referred to as the "Western Captivity" of Orthodox theology. While the extent of Roman Catholic influence has no doubt been exaggerated, it cannot be denied that both Russian and Greek theological works of the last centuries bear the marks of Latin influence. For example, one needs only to recall the often repeated statement that the Orthodox Church recognizes "seven sacraments." The enumeration of seven sacraments is the product of medieval Roman Catholic theology, not Orthodox theology.

The Latin influence on Orthodox theology is most clearly seen, however, in the way theological books are organized. The most complete theological manual available in English is Fr. Michael Pomazansky's *Orthodox Dogmatic Theology*. This is a marvellous book, which I highly recommend as a reference tool. However, it is not without problems.

Orthodox Dogmatic Theology begins with a discussion of the sources of revelation and proceeds to a discussion of the nature and attributes of God, all before in-

PREFACE

troducing the doctrine of the Trinity. Although the content of the book is thoroughly Orthodox, the material is presented in a manner no different from that of Roman Catholic or Protestant manuals of theology.

The present catechism presupposes that the *way* the teachings of the Church are explained is important. Orthodox theology is an organic whole. Every aspect of the life of the Church is an expression of the life of the Holy Trinity, made accessible to man through the Incarnation of the Son of God. *The Faith* is designed to express that fundamental unity. No topic is considered in isolation. Everything revolves around the fundamental doctrines of the Trinity and the Incarnation.

I owe a great debt of gratitude to Frank Schaeffer for making the publication of this volume possible and to William Anderson for editing it. I also wish to thank the members of the Editorial Committee for their input and corrections. It is a rather daunting task to produce a book entitled *The Faith*—one which should be undertaken only with fear and trembling. It is, therefore, a great blessing to have the oversight of these venerable hierarchs, especially that of my own beloved archpastor, Archbishop Dmitri of Dallas.

Clark (Innocent) Carlton
Feast of the Lord's Baptism
1997

INTRODUCTION
What is the Orthodox Church?

The Orthodox Church is the original Christian Church, established by our Lord Jesus Christ upon the foundation of the Apostles, Himself being the chief Cornerstone, and enlivened by the Holy Spirit on the Day of Pentecost.

In 1987, almost 2,000 evangelical Christians in various cities throughout the United States converted *en masse* to the Orthodox Church. Since that time several Protestant congregations have converted, as well as thousands of individuals. A Church known for its antiquity and adherence to tradition is now one of the fastest growing Christian groups in America. What is the attraction of Orthodoxy? Why are so many people leaving the religion of their upbringing to embrace this ancient faith?

In 1794, monks from the Valaam Monastery in northwestern Russia were sent as missionaries to Russian Alaska. There, for the first time, the peoples of North America heard the Christian Gospel in all of its apostolic fullness. There, for the first time, converts

INTRODUCTION

were baptized and the Eucharist was celebrated in what is now the state of Alaska.

Although Orthodoxy has been on this continent for two centuries, it remains little known. For many, it is simply an exotic, eastern version of Roman Catholicism. For others, it is mainly associated with Greek or Russian or Middle Eastern food festivals. A great many more Americans do not even realize that the Orthodox Church exists.

Perhaps the greatest tragedy in all of this is that many Orthodox Christians themselves do not know much about their faith. It is not unheard of for an Orthodox Christian to describe his faith as "Catholicism without the Pope."

There is, of course, a reason for this unfortunate situation. Although the first priests in North America came here specifically as missionaries, the vast majority of Orthodox Churches in the continental United States were founded by immigrants from Greece, Eastern Europe, and the Middle East. For the most part, these Christians worshipped in the language of their mother country. This helped to insulate the community from the wider American society, and, as a result, insulated society from the treasures of the Church.

With the mass conversion of the "Evangelical Orthodox" in 1987, however, the cat was out of the bag. The Orthodox Church is experiencing a great renewal in this country. Not only are thousands of Americans turning to the Orthodox Church as their true spiritual home, many of those reared in the Church have rediscovered the rich treasure of Orthodoxy.

WHAT IS THE ORTHODOX CHURCH?

The reason for this renewal is clear: People are finding in Orthodoxy the fullness of the apostolic faith. Tired of following this new religious leader or that new fad, they are looking for a Church with deep, historical roots. They are also tired of having the doctrinal rug pulled out from under them by their own pastors and bishops. They are looking for a faith that does not change with the weather. People are also hungry for genuine worship, a real encounter with God and not merely a lecture or emotional pep-rally. Finally, people are looking for evidence of genuine sanctity. They want a religion that makes a difference in their lives, not just an interesting theological system.

The Orthodox Church is all of this and more, for She is nothing less than *the* Church, founded by our Lord Jesus Christ. Although the Orthodox Church judges the soul of no man, leaving judgment solely to God, She does claim that She, and She alone, is the one, holy, catholic, and apostolic Church confessed in the Nicene Creed.

The claim of the Orthodox Church to be the one and only *true* Church is based upon four factors:

1. The Orthodox Church has maintained an unbroken historical continuity with the original Church founded by Jesus in Jerusalem.

2. The Orthodox Church has faithfully maintained the apostolic faith *once delivered to the Saints* (Jude 3), neither adding to nor subtracting from it.

3. The Orthodox Church faithfully worships God the Father in Spirit and in Truth, providing man-

INTRODUCTION

kind with personal access to the life and grace of the All-holy Trinity.

4. The Orthodox Church has produced untold numbers of Saints throughout the centuries—persons who bear within themselves the uncreated grace of God.

Historical Continuity

Compared with European countries, the United States is a relatively young nation. For most of us, however, this fact goes unnoticed. Indeed, anyone who visits Philadelphia or Williamsburg gets a definite sense of American history. It is not until one travels to Europe and climbs around castles built centuries before Columbus' voyage or perhaps stays in a inn built decades before the American Revolution that one begins to realize just how young our own country really is.

It is much the same with religion. The typical American Christian has very little, if any, historical consciousness. He may know a few things about the history of his denomination, but it is not until he is confronted with a church of great antiquity that he begins to consider the origins of his own faith. When encountering the Orthodox Church, the Protestant Christian comes face to face with a form of Christianity three times as old as his own.

The origin of most Protestant denominations can be traced back to one or two founders. Thus, the Lutheran Church is traced back to Martin Luther, the Reformed

WHAT IS THE ORTHODOX CHURCH?

Church to John Calvin, the Presbyterian Church to John Knox, the Methodist Church to the Wesleys (although they never actually left the Anglican Church), and the Churches of Christ to Barton Stone and Alexander Campbell. Although Baptist Churches cannot claim one founder, their history is traceable through the English Separatist Movement back to the Church of England. In every case, the trail stops dead in the sixteenth century with the Protestant Reformation.

The Orthodox Church, in contrast, traces its history back to the first century Church of Jerusalem, founded by Christ Himself. The Church is fully conscious of this history. Indeed, She celebrates it, marking important events in Her history throughout the year with special celebrations.

This concern with history is an important element of the Orthodox Faith, for it underscores the fact that the Church is an historical community. When Christ ascended to heaven, He did not leave behind a system of philosophy or a school. He left His Church, which was a concrete, historical community there in Jerusalem. From Jerusalem, the Christian Gospel spread throughout the known world, and local Churches were created. All of these local Churches, however, sprang from and were dependent upon the original Church in Jerusalem for their faith and practice.

Christianity is not a philosophy; it is not a set of rules that one may follow on one's own. It is a life which can only be lived in community, in the Church that Christ Himself founded. Our Lord made it perfectly clear that this Church would overcome the gates

INTRODUCTION

of hell itself. So the question that faces the modern Christian is, "Which community is the authentic Church?"

The Orthodox Church of today does not *imitate* that original Christian community; She *is* that community. When the "Evangelical Orthodox" first began their pilgrimage from Evangelical Protestantism to Orthodoxy, they called themselves the "New Covenant Apostolic Order." They tried as best they could to make their communities *like* the Church they read about in the New Testament. As the years went on, however, they realized that imitation was not enough. They found that the Church they were trying to imitate still existed, and that authentic Christianity could be lived only within Her embrace.

The historical continuity of the Orthodox Church, therefore, is the first pillar of Her claim to be the one, authentic Church of Christ. Others may try to imitate the Church of the New Testament, some more closely than others, but no Protestant denomination can claim an organic unity with Her.

Apostolic Doctrine

Historical continuity by itself, however, is not enough to ensure that a community is the true Church. The Orthodox Church is the true Church of Christ not only because She can trace Her history uninterruptedly back to the New Testament, but also because She has faithfully maintained the authentic teaching of the Apostles, neither adding to nor subtracting from it.

WHAT IS THE ORTHODOX CHURCH?

The Roman Catholic Church can also claim an unbroken, historical succession from the time of the Apostles down to today, yet Rome has changed the teaching of the early Church on important issues and added strange doctrines of its own invention. For these reasons the Orthodox Church is not in communion with Rome, there being no unity of life without unity of faith.

In the eleventh century, the Church of Rome officially altered the Nicene Creed. This alteration had been refused by Popes until that time. When, however, the alteration was made official, the Church of Rome no longer confessed the same faith as the early Church.

Another difference between the Orthodox and Roman Catholic Churches concerns the authority of the Pope. From the eleventh century on, the Papacy made increasingly bold claims to sovereignty over the entire Church, including the other patriarchs—claims *never* accepted by Eastern bishops and *never* affirmed by an Ecumenical Council. This trend reached its apex with the First Vatican Council (19th c.). This Roman council decreed as a dogma of the Roman Church that the Pope is infallible when he speaks *ex cathedra,* that is, in his official capacity as Pope.

The idea that any one individual in the Church is infallible is blatantly absurd. In the early Church, when problems arose over doctrine or discipline, the Apostles, and later the bishops whom they appointed, met together in councils to decide these issues.

In Acts 15 we read of the first Church council, which was held in Jerusalem. The question was raised

INTRODUCTION

whether gentile converts to Christianity should be circumcised. Peter, Paul, and Barnabas addressed the assembly, then James, the Bishop of Jerusalem, summed up the proceedings and issued a judgment with which all agreed. They announced their decision with the words, *It seemed good to the Holy Spirit and to us...*

No individual member of the Church can lay special claim to the Holy Spirit. Issues have always been decided by the whole body of the Church meeting in council. This spirit of collegiality (in Russian, *sobornost*) is the Church's safeguard against heresy, for many bishops have gone astray and taught heresy. Patriarch Nestorius of Constantinople (5th c.) was deposed and condemned as a heretic by the Third Ecumenical Council. Pope Honorius of Rome (7th c.) was condemned as a heretic by the Sixth Ecumenical Council. Interestingly, until the eleventh century, when Papal claims began to snowball, all Popes had to affirm their allegiance to the Sixth Council and its condemnation of Pope Honorius as part of their oath of office.

Church history is a messy business. It is full of heresies and schisms. Sometimes these issues took centuries to resolve. The Orthodox Church makes no attempt sweep this under the rug. There is no attempt to pretend that Nestorius was not Patriarch of Constantinople; he was, and he was a heretic. The point is, however, that he was deposed from office and his teachings condemned.

The Orthodox Church teaches the same things today that it did in the year 1000, the same things it taught in the year 100; there is a perfect continuity of faith and life. This is easily contrasted not only with the novel teachings of the Roman Catholic Church, but with the doctrines of the various Protestant denominations. All Protestant sects have changed considerably since their founding. Many denominations do not even teach the same things they taught fifty years ago, much less four hundred years ago. It is safe to say, for example, that John Wesley would not recognize much of what goes on today by the name of Methodism.

E. Y. Mullins, one of the most prominent Baptist theologians of this century, once said that theology had to be reinvented every generation. This is absolute nonsense. The Apostle Paul warns of those who would change the message of the Gospel and clearly commands us: *Therefore, brethren, stand fast, and hold the traditions which ye have been taught, whether by word, or our epistle* (2 Thessalonians 2:15).

The Orthodox Christian is not free to believe whatever he wants to believe or interpret the Holy Scripture in whatever way strikes his fancy. Nor are bishops free to teach whatever they want. All are called to accept and live by the apostolic tradition, which has been handed down uncorrupt from the first century until today.

Right Worship

The word *Orthodox* means both right belief and right glory or worship. For the Orthodox, worship and doctrine are inseparable. The proper worship of God must be rooted in a proper understanding of Who He

INTRODUCTION

is. Conversely, a flawed understanding of God will inevitably lead to improper worship, which insults rather than glorifies the All-holy Trinity.

When God gave the Law to Moses for the People of Israel, He not only gave the Ten Commandments as an ethical guide, He also gave very specific instructions as to how He was to be worshipped. Failure to follow those rules could have terrible consequences, as Korah and his followers discovered when they "illegally" offered incense. The ground opened up and swallowed some, while others were consumed by fire from heaven:

> *And Eleazar the priest took the brazen censers, wherewith they that were burnt had offered; and they were made broad plates for a covering of the altar: to be a memorial unto the Children of Israel, that no stranger, which is not of the seed of Aaron, come near to offer incense before the Lord; that he be not as Korah and as his company: as the Lord said to him by the hand of Moses* (Numbers 16:39-40).

The "ministers" of the Old Testament were not set apart to minister to the people, but to God, Who was objectively present in the tabernacle and, later, the temple. This concept of ministry was adopted by the New Testament Church, which was, after all, composed at first entirely of Jews. The early Church adopted, with appropriate changes, the Jewish liturgical day, beginning at sundown, set times of prayer (Acts 2:42), the yearly calendar of fasts and feasts (Acts 20:16), and, most importantly, the belief that worship is a sacrifice directed toward God (Hebrews 13:15).

WHAT IS THE ORTHODOX CHURCH?

Since the time of the Protestant Reformation, however, the idea of worship as a sacrifice and ministration unto God has been gradually replaced with the notion of congregation-centered worship, where the clergy minister to the people rather than to God. The result is a plethora of "worship services," which range from dry lectures to variety show productions to religious pep-rallies.

The basic pattern of Orthodox services, on the other hand, has not changed substantially since their inception. To be sure, as the Church went from a persecuted sect to a legalized religion and finally to the official religion of the Roman Empire, the services became more elaborate and complicated. It is only natural that the services conducted in a great cathedral like that of Hagia Sophia in Constantinople would be more elaborate than those conducted in secret in a believer's living room in Judea. However, the basic structure remained the same. The Divine Liturgy celebrated in an Orthodox Church today is structurally the same service as that described by St. Justin the Philosopher in the year 150:

> And on the day which is called the Sun's Day there is an assembly of all who live in the towns or country; and the memoirs of the Apostles or the writings of the prophets are read, as much as time permits. When the reader has finished, the president gives a discourse, admonishing us and exhorting us to imitate these excellent examples. Then we all rise together and offer prayers; and, as I said above, on the conclusion of our prayer, bread is brought and wine and water; and the president similarly offers

INTRODUCTION

up prayers and thanksgivings (literally "eucharists") to the best of his power, and the people assent with *Amen*. Then follows the distribution of the Eucharistic Gifts and the partaking of them by all; and they are sent to the absent by the hands of the deacons (*Apology* I).

The Church is first and foremost a worshipping community, gathered around the Table of Her Lord, offering to Him in sacrifice the substance of Her life on earth (bread and wine) and receiving these Gifts back from Him as the Body and Blood of Christ. St. Nicholas Cabasilas sums up the importance of the Church's worship:

> It appears therefore, that to worship God *in Spirit and in Truth* (John 4:24) and to offer Him pure homage is an effect of the Holy Table. From this mystery, therefore, we obtain the gift of being Christ's members and thus of being like Him. While we were dead it was impossible to offer homage to the living God. But unless we constantly feast at the Banquet it is impossible to be alive and to be released from dead works. Just as *God is spirit, and those who worship Him must worship Him in Spirit and in Truth* (John 4:24), so it is fitting that those who choose to worship the Living One should themselves be living, for, as He says, *He is not God of the dead, but of the living* (Matthew 22:32) (*The Life in Christ*).

True Sanctity

Historical continuity, apostolic doctrine, and right worship are central to the claim of the Orthodox

WHAT IS THE ORTHODOX CHURCH?

Church to be the authentic Church of Christ. These elements mean little, however, if lives are not changed, if men and women are not conformed to the image of Christ. In other words, the proof is in the final product. Archimandrite Vasileios of the Iveron Monastery on Mt. Athos writes:

> In the same way, faithfulness to the tradition and the dogmatic teaching of the Church means not only that the right formulations of terms are not altered, but also that our lives are altered and renewed by the truth and regenerative power latent in those terms. Then man acquires senses and is able to see; he becomes conscious of the deeper meaning and value of the Orthodox faith as a force in life (*Hymn of Entry*, p. 19).

Since the first century, the Orthodox Church has produced countless thousands of true Saints. It is important to note, however, that a Saint is not simply a nice, moral person. It is not necessary to be a Christian in order to be a morally upstanding citizen. Mormons are some of the nicest, most moral people you could ever meet, but they are not Christians. A Saint, on the other hand, is one whose life has been totally transformed by the uncreated grace of the Holy Trinity into the likeness of the Son of God.

St. Nectarios of Pentapolis was born to a poor, Greek family but quickly rose to the rank of metropolitan in the Church of Alexandria, Egypt. Known for his strict asceticism and his love for the poor and downtrodden, he was well loved by the common people. This, however, aroused great jealousy on the part of the

INTRODUCTION

other clerics in the Patriarchate. They embarked on a smear campaign against him, and he was fired from his position. Even after he returned to Greece, his enemies did not leave him alone, stirring up trouble and false allegations against him wherever he went.

After many years at the helm of the Rizarios School in Athens, he moved to the island of Aegina and founded a women's monastery. Even in old age, however, his enemies did not leave him alone. He continued to have problems with Church officials, and at one point he was visited by a civil prosecutor who made the absurd claim that he was keeping a harem and dumping the bodies of his bastard children down a well.

Through all of these trials and persecutions, however, God was refining the soul of His servant as gold is purified in a fire (cf. 1 Peter 1:7). St. Nectarios became so humble, so utterly dependent upon His Creator, that the uncreated grace of God literally overflowed his frail body. He was known to be clairvoyant, and many sought his prayers, knowing that *the effectual fervent prayer of a righteous man availeth much* (James 5:16).

St. Nectarios died in an Athens hospital in 1920. The nun and nurse who were attending him removed his woolen undershirt and carelessly tossed it onto the bed of a paralytic. The paralyzed man immediately stood up and began praising God. The next day, at the first public viewing of his body, the crowd was amazed to see that his face was exuding a sweet-smelling myrrh.

Six months later his coffin was opened while work was being done to the grave. St. Nectarios' unembalmed body had remained uncorrupt and continued to exude myrrh. Like the bones of the prophet Elisha that brought a dead man to life (2 Kings 13:21), the body of St. Nectarios became a source of healing and spiritual power. God's power and majesty are manifest in His Saints even in death.

A Saint, therefore, is not simply a good person. A Saint is one whose life has been so transformed by the grace of God that he or she radiates that grace to those around. A Saint is one who has attained, insofar as it is possible in this life, the likeness of God within himself. In the final analysis, a Saint is the living embodiment of the history, doctrine, worship, and ethical life of the Church.

The life of a true Saint of God such as St. Nectarios is easily contrasted with what so often passes for "spirituality" in our society. Ours is a generation which seeks after signs and wonders (cf. Matthew 12:39) and places tremendous emphasis on religious "experiences." Yet, outside the Church there are very few genuine yardsticks against which one can measure these experiences. The devil often appears as an angel of light (cf. 2 Corinthians 11:14); so how is one to know if an experience or spiritual "technique" is helpful or harmful?

Let us consider one of the most controversial forms of contemporary religious experience: holy laughter. Holy laughter is a nationwide religious phenomenon that grew out of a Charismatic, Protestant revival in Canada known as the "Toronto Blessing." During services people in the congregation begin laughing uncontrollably, even to the point of incapacitation. Occasion-

INTRODUCTION

ally some will drop to the floor on their hands and knees and begin to make animal noises such as barking like a dog. All of this is said to be done "in the Spirit."

Holy laughter is highly controversial, even within Charismatic and Pentecostal circles. Nevertheless, practitioners come armed to the teeth with a slew of supporting Bible verses and the insistence that such experiences draw them closer to God. For many, the positive emotional impact of the practice is enough to confirm its "Christian" character.

For the Orthodox Christian, however, holy laughter is simply not an issue. He has at his disposal almost two thousand years of Church history and the detailed doctrinal teachings of the Church against which to measure such phenomena. In the services of Vespers, Matins, and the Divine Liturgy, he experiences true worship and communion with God and is able to intuit immediately when something is amiss or unseemly. Finally, he has literally thousands of Saints as examples of genuine sanctity.

The lives of the Saints are full of stories of people laughing uncontrollably or making animal noises. In *all* cases, the cause was demonic activity. Much of the holy laughter movement may be nothing more than mass hysteria, an explainable psychological phenomenon. Where spirits are involved in this movement, however, it is perfectly clear in the light of Church history, doctrine, liturgy, and the lives of the Saints that the spirits are demonic.

The Orthodox Christian makes this judgment on the basis of neither abstract theories nor his own lim-

WHAT IS THE ORTHODOX CHURCH?

ited, individual experience, but upon the corporate experience of the Church. When Treasury officers are trained to spot counterfeit money, they are shown only real currency. They learn to distinguish the genuine from the false because they learn the earmarks of the genuine currency so well. Such is the case with the Orthodox Christian.

* * *

History, doctrine, worship, and spirituality are all different aspects of the apostolic tradition. None is sufficient of itself without the others. Right belief without an organic, historical connection with the New Testament Church is merely to imitate the past without sharing in its ongoing life, to have the *form of godliness, but denying the power thereof* (2 Timothy 3:5). On the other hand, to have an unbroken historical connection without preserving the Apostles' doctrine can only result in improper worship and false spirituality. Archimandrite Vasileios writes,

> Only when we are conformed to Christ, recognizing Him by partaking in His life, do we "regain our proper stature," our natural function and our freedom, as the Church and as persons. Ecclesiology and spirituality have the same basis: dogma. The Church is Christ, His Body living in history. It is summarized in each of the faithful, who is the Church in miniature. The personal consciousness of each of the faithful has an ecclesial dimension, and every problem for the Church is the problem of the

INTRODUCTION

personal salvation of each of the faithful (*Hymn of Entry*, pp. 20-21).

The Apostle Paul referred to the Church as *the pillar and ground of the truth* (1 Timothy 3:15) and as the Body of Christ, *the fullness of Him that filleth all in all* (Ephesians 1:23). The Orthodox Christian experiences this fullness. There is nothing in the Church that is lacking for his salvation.

Every day in Her liturgical gatherings—and especially on Sundays—the Church commemorates the lives of various Saints. The whole Church of Christ, both on earth and in heaven, gathers around the Throne of Glory to offer the Father true worship in Spirit and in Truth. The Divine Scriptures are read and explained; the unchangeable doctrines are expressed in hymns, and the lives of the Saints are given as examples to emulate. The faithful are then invited to the one Cup, which is communion with Christ Himself (cf. 1 Corinthians 10:16).

What is the Orthodox Church? Above all, She is life in Christ, our participation in and through Him in the unending life of the All-holy Trinity. In the Church we are prepared for the life of the age to come not only by being taught the commandments of Christ but by actively experiencing His grace. St. Nicholas Cabasilas summed up the life of the Church in this way:

> As nature prepares the fetus, while it is in its dark and fluid life, for that life which is in the light, and shapes it, as though according to a model, for the life which it is about to receive, so likewise it happens to the Saints. This is what the Apostle Paul

WHAT IS THE ORTHODOX CHURCH?

said when he wrote to the Galatians, *my little children, with whom I am again in travail until Christ be formed in you* (Galatians 4:19).

. . . For us, too, that Sun has graciously risen, the heavenly fragrance has been poured forth into the malodorous places, and the Bread of angels has been given even unto men.

This is the way in which we draw this life into our souls—by being initiated into the mysteries, being washed and anointed and partaking of the Holy Table. . . . O how great is His goodness! He crowns those who have been washed, and those who partake of His Banquet He proclaims victors (*The Life in Christ*).

The Symbol of Faith

I believe in one God, the Father Almighty, Maker of heaven and earth and of all things visible and invisible.

And in one Lord, Jesus Christ, the Son of God, the Only-begotten, begotten of the Father before all ages; Light of Light, very God of very God; begotten, not made; of one essence with the Father; by Whom all things were made; Who, for us men and for our salvation, came down from heaven and was incarnate of the Holy Spirit and the Virgin Mary, and was made man. And He was crucified also for us under Pontius Pilate, suffered and was buried. And the third day He rose again according to the Scriptures, and ascended into heaven, and sitteth on the right hand of the Father. And He shall come again with glory to judge the living and the dead; Whose kingdom shall have no end.

And in the Holy Spirit, the Lord, the Giver of Life, Who proceedeth from the Father, Who with the Father and Son together is worshipped and glorified, Who spoke by the prophets.

I believe in one, holy, catholic, and apostolic Church. I confess one Baptism for the remission of sins. I look for the resurrection of the dead, and the life of the age to come. Amen.

Part One

The Doctrines of Christ

CHAPTER ONE

The Foundation of the Orthodox Faith

As the Body of Christ, the Church is mankind's participation in the unending life of the Holy Trinity.

"God became man so that man might become God"—this famous saying by St. Athanasius of Alexandria (4th c.) sums up the message of Orthodoxy. God created mankind in His own image so that mankind might become like God, sharing in His eternal, divine life. God's good will toward His creatures was not limited to the act of creation, however. Seeing that man was unable to realize the likeness of God in himself because of his sinfulness, God sent His own Son, the *very Image of His person* (Hebrews 1:3), into the world to take human nature upon Himself and restore it to its original glory in the image of God. In other words, God—the Creator of all things—became man so that we might become like Him. In the words of the Liturgy of St. Basil, "He emptied Himself, taking the form of a servant, being likened to the body of our lowliness, that He might liken us to the image of His glory." This is known as *theosis*—or deification. This is why the world

is Orthodox theosis consistent with Catholicism?

CHAPTER ONE

was created. This is why you were born. This is the truth of Orthodoxy.

But what does it mean to become like God or to be a *partaker of the divine nature* (2 Peter 1:4)? When the Church answers this question She is engaging in "theology," which literally means "a word about God." The Church is able to make statements about God because God has revealed Himself to mankind. Through His act of creation, through His many acts of mercy and displays of power throughout history, as recorded in the Bible, and especially in the sending of His Son, Jesus Christ, God has made Himself known to those whom He had created in His own image.

Thus, the Church's theology — what She says about God — is based upon what God has revealed about Himself. For this reason, when the Church answers the question, "What does it mean to become like God?" She does not look to the theories of modern psychology or sociology for the answer. Rather, She turns to the teachings and life of Her Lord: *All things are delivered unto Me of My Father: and no man knoweth the Son, but the Father; neither knoweth any man the Father, save the Son, and he to whomsoever the Son will reveal Him* (Matthew 11:27).

The foundation of everything the Church believes and teaches is the fact that God is not some impersonal essence or philosophical principle, but the Father Who exists in an eternal communion of love with His Son and His Spirit and Who speaks to those whom He has created *face to face, as a man speaketh unto his friend* (Exodus 33:11). A person, as opposed to an individual, exists only in relationship to other persons. For God this relationship is eternal, for the Father is never without His Son and His Spirit. Love is not an attribute or characteristic of God; it defines His very being. *God is love* (1 John 4:8). This is the meaning of the doctrine of the Trinity.

According to the Book of Genesis, mankind was created in the image of God—this God of personal love. Thus, we too are inherently personal beings. We were created to love as God Himself loves: *Beloved, let us love one another: for love is of God; and every one that loveth is born of God, and knoweth God* (1 John 4:7). Our creation in the image of God is the foundation of our very being and determines the purpose of our existence. This means that for man to be truly human—to be what he was created to be—he must attain unto the likeness of the Holy Trinity. "Man," says St. Basil the Great (4th c.), "is a creature with orders to become God."

It is clear, however, that mankind has failed miserably in its divinely appointed task. Instead of growing in the likeness of God, we have cast ourselves into the likeness of the devil. We have used our Godlike freedom to turn away from Him, rather than toward Him in love. Man, of himself, cannot bridge the gap between his creatureliness and the uncreated glory of God. Nor can he remove the effects of his own sinfulness. In short, mankind is incapable of becoming what it was created to be: a participant in the life of the Holy Trinity.

If mankind could not ascend to heaven and unite itself with God, then it remained for God to come down

CHAPTER ONE

to earth and unite Himself with mankind. Jesus Christ—the eternal Son and Word of God—became man and lived a human life so that mankind might fulfill the end for which it was created: union with God. *And the Word was made flesh, and dwelt among us, and we beheld His glory, the glory as of the Only-begotten of the Father, full of grace and truth* (John 1:14). This is the meaning of the doctrine of the Incarnation: that the Word of God became fully human without ceasing to be fully God.

By taking our humanity upon Himself, God also assumed all of the consequences of our sinfulness. It was not enough that He merely appear as man or that He take upon Himself only the higher aspects of our nature, for as St. Gregory the Theologian (4th c.) said, "What is not assumed is not healed." To heal and redeem fallen humanity, Christ had to enter into the lowest depths of human existence and break the stranglehold of sin and death upon the human race. This is the significance of the Cross: the Son of God descended into the pit of hades in order to lead mankind up to the heights of heaven. St. Mark the Ascetic (5th c.) wrote, "All the penalties imposed by divine judgment upon man for the sin of the first transgression—death, toil, hunger, thirst, and the like—He took upon Himself, becoming what we are, so that we might become what He is."

The Incarnation, therefore, is mankind's passage from death to life. In uniting our humanity to Himself, the Son of God presents us to His Father, and we share in the life of the Holy Trinity:

THE FOUNDATION OF THE ORTHODOX FAITH

But when the fullness of time was come, God sent forth His Son, made of a woman, made under the law, to redeem them that were under the law, that we might receive the adoption of sons. And because ye are sons, God hath sent forth the Spirit of His Son into your hearts, crying, "Abba, Father" (Galatians 4:4-6).

United with the eternal Son of God through the power of the Holy Spirit, we are able to stand before God our Creator and say, "Our Father, Who art in heaven..."

The work that Christ accomplished once and for all in Palestine almost 2000 years ago is not limited to people who lived back then, for Christ assumed our human nature in its entirety and placed it on the Throne of God at the Father's right hand. Christ was not simply an individual, unrelated to the rest of us, nor did He cease being human after His Resurrection and Ascension to the Father. In other words, although the Incarnation had a beginning in time — the Annunciation to the Virgin Mary and her conception of Christ — it has no ending. It is possible for every human being to share in the life of the Holy Trinity by being united to Christ, because He has already united Himself to us and has promised to abide with us forever.

For us to experience the life of the Trinity, however, we must live the life that Christ came to give us. That is, we must allow His humanity to become our humanity, transforming us by the power of the Holy Spirit into His very Body. St. Paul calls the Church "the Body of Christ" and explains how we, as different human beings, can become one body with Christ:

CHAPTER ONE

For as the body is one, and hath many members, and all the members of that one body, being many, are one body: so also is Christ. For by one Spirit are we all baptized into one Body, whether we be Jews or Gentiles, whether we be bond or free, and have been all made to drink into one Spirit (1 Corinthians 12:12-13).

Thus, the Body of Christ is Christ's continuing presence here on earth and mankind's participation in His work of salvation. In other words, the Church is the continuation of the Incarnation. By sharing in the life of the Church, we participate in the life of Christ. His life then becomes our life: *I am crucified with Christ nevertheless I live, yet not I, but Christ liveth in me: and the life I now live in the flesh I live by faith in the Son of God, Who loved me, and gave Himself for me* (Galatians 2:20). Unless we willingly partake of Christ's life, we have no hope of eternal life; for it is only through Him that we are united with God the Father:

> *I am the living Bread which came down from heaven: if any man eat of this Bread, he shall live forever; and the Bread that I will give is My Flesh, which I will give for the life of the world. . . . Verily, verily, I say unto you, except ye eat the Flesh of the Son of Man, and drink His Blood, ye have no life in you. . . . He that eateth My Flesh, and drinketh My Blood dwelleth in Me and I in him. As the living Father hath sent Me, and I live by the Father: so he that eateth Me, even he shall live by Me* (John 6:51, 53, 56-57).

As the sacrament of Christ's presence, the Church is not primarily an institution, but a life: the life of the Holy Trinity made accessible to man. Therefore, everything that the Church does is a sacrament. That is, it is

THE FOUNDATION OF THE ORTHODOX FAITH

both the revelation of the life of the Holy Trinity to man and man's participation in that divine life. Nothing which directly pertains to the life of the Church is in any way accidental or unimportant. Everything within the Church works together to sing the same hymn of praise: "Holy, Holy, Holy, Lord of Hosts, heaven and earth are full of Thy glory!" All that the Church is and all that She does proclaims the dogma of the Holy Trinity and invites mankind to fulfill its destiny in the likeness of the God of Love.

The foundation of the Orthodox Faith—the absolute bedrock of our salvation—is the Trinity and the Incarnation. If God is not the God of Love, then there is truly no purpose for our existence, for "between the Trinity and hell there lies no other choice" (Vladimir Lossky). If Christ is not God made man, then there is no hope for our salvation, for mankind could never share in the life of God had God not first taken upon Himself the life of man. The Trinity and the Incarnation: everything in the Church revolves around these two doctrines. In short, the Church is the incarnation of the life of the Holy Trinity; the Church is the experience of salvation itself.

THE FATHERS SPEAK

Here, then, is the plan of our faith, the foundation of the building and the glue of our way of life. The first article is: God the Father, uncreated, indescribable, invisible, one God, the Creator of all things.

CHAPTER ONE

The second article is: the Word of God, the Son of God, Christ Jesus our Lord, Who was set forth by the prophets, each contributing his share of the prophecy, according to the plan of the Father, and through Him all things were made. Now, in the fullness of time, in order to sum up all things in Himself, He has become a man among humans, visible and tangible, in order to abolish death, show forth life, and establish communion between God and man.

The third article is: The Holy Spirit, through Whom the prophets prophesied, the fathers were taught the things of God, and the righteous were led in the way of righteousness. In the fullness of time He has been poured out in a new way upon humanity everywhere, renewing us to God.

> **St. Irenaios of Lyons**
> from *The Preaching of the Apostles*
> Tr. by Jack N. Sparks
> Holy Cross Orthodox Press, 1987

Trinity beyond all being, worshipped in Unity, take from me the heavy yoke of sin, and in Thy compassion grant me tears of compunction.

O Virgin inviolate and Mother who hast not known man, from thee has God, the Creator of the ages, taken human flesh, uniting to Himself the nature of men.

> **St. Andrew of Crete**
> from *The Great Canon*
> *The Lenten Triodion*
> Tr. by Mother Mary and K.T. Ware
> Faber and Faber, 1977

THE FOUNDATION OF THE ORTHODOX FAITH
Special Study
The Sign of the Cross

The most common act of devotion for an Orthodox Christian is to make the sign of the Cross. This is done by bringing the thumb and first two fingers of the right hand together and tucking the remaining two fingers into the palm. Then we bless ourselves in a crosswise fashion, touching the forehead, breast, right shoulder, and then the left.

Unfortunately, many people do not fully appreciate the significance of this action. The non-Orthodox do not understand such physical acts of devotion and often look upon the sign of the Cross as some sort of empty ritual or even as a "good-luck charm." Sadly, even many Orthodox Christians use the sign in a haphazard manner, paying little attention to the proper outward form or to the inner meaning. The sign of the Cross, however, should not simply be brushed aside as a piece of optional piety, for by this little gesture the Christian sums up the entire teaching of the Church.

By bringing the thumb and the first two fingers of the right hand together, we signify the doctrine of the Trinity. In doing so, we confess that we believe not in an impersonal being, but in a personal God—the God who *is* Love. We confess that we believe in and worship the Father, the Son, and the Holy Spirit: three co-eternal and co-equal persons in one undivided Godhead.

CHAPTER ONE

By tucking the remaining two fingers into the palm, we signify the doctrine of the Incarnation. In this way we confess that God has become man—that the Second Person of the Holy Trinity took upon Himself our humanity while remaining God from all eternity. Thus, we confess that Christ is *both* fully God and fully man—not 50% God and 50% man, but 100% God and 100% man.

Furthermore, by making the sign of the Cross in this way, we confess the depth of the love of God toward us. For by dying on the Cross, Jesus Christ—One of the Holy Trinity—took upon Himself the ultimate consequence of man's Fall—death itself—in order to raise us up and give us the eternal life of the Holy Trinity. By touching the forehead, breast, and shoulders, we commend our mind, our heart, and our strength to the power of the precious and life-giving Cross, and we remind ourselves that we must take up our *own* Cross and follow our Lord:

> Rejoice! Cross of the Lord: through thee mankind has been delivered from the curse. Shattering the enemy by thine Exaltation, O Cross all-venerable, thou art a sign of true joy. Thou art our help, thou art the strength of kings, the power of righteous men, the majesty of priests. All who sign themselves with thee are freed from peril. Thou rod of strength under which we like sheep are tended, thou art a weapon of peace round which the angels stand in fear. Thou art the divine glory of Christ, Who grants the world great mercy (*The Festal Menaion*).

THE FOUNDATION OF THE ORTHODOX FAITH

Orthodox Christians begin each day with the sign of the Cross and the invocation of the All-holy Trinity. Furthermore, we should sign ourselves with the Cross not only at the beginning of our prayers but also before beginning any task. In this way, we commend each and every moment of the day to the All-holy Trinity and the protection of the Holy Cross of our Lord.

When the bishop serves at the Liturgy, he blesses the faithful with the sign of the Cross in a special way. He holds a three-branched candlestick, called a *trikirion*, in his right hand and a two-branched candlestick, called a *dikirion*, in his left. With these he blesses the People of God in a crosswise fashion. In the person of her sacramental head, the bishop, the Church confesses her unwavering faith in all that the Holy Trinity has done for the salvation of mankind. By this all of the faithful are blessed, for they are guarded by the power of the Cross in the worship of the undivided Trinity and in the confession that Jesus Christ—God made man—is the Lord of all.

CHAPTER ONE
Reflection

1. Why did God create mankind?

2. How does the Christian understanding of God differ from that of other religions?

3. What does the nature of God tell us about human nature?

4. What has God done to reverse the effects of man's sin and restore him to fellowship with Himself?

5. What did Christ come to give to mankind?

6. What did St. Paul call the Church?

7. In what way is the Church related to the Incarnation of the Son of God?

8. What does the Church have to do with the life of the Holy Trinity?

9. Can man share in the life of Christ or the Father apart from the Church?

10. What two doctrines are the foundation of the Orthodox Faith?

Chapter Two
The Holy Trinity

God is not an impersonal concept or an isolated individual, but the Father Who exists in an eternal communion of love with His Son and His Spirit.

Vladimir Lossky wrote, "The Trinity is, for the Orthodox Church, the unshakable foundation of all religious thought, of all piety, of all spiritual life, of all experience. It is the Trinity that we seek in seeking after God, when we search for the fullness of being, for the end and meaning of existence" (*The Mystical Theology of the Eastern Church*, p. 65). The dogma of the Trinity is the most difficult teaching of the Church to grasp because it transcends the capabilities of our limited, human reason. No matter how hard we try, we cannot make $1+1+1=1$. And yet, the Church confesses precisely this: that there are three co-equal and co-eternal persons in one undivided Godhead, and that these three persons are one God and not three. This is why Lossky described the doctrine of the Trinity as "a cross for human ways of thought."

But why do we need to believe in the Trinity? The Church proclaims the dogma of the Trinity because it is *true*, and truth is the Church's only concern. As Archi-

CHAPTER TWO

mandrite Vasileios says in the *Hymn of Entry*, "The Lord came, not to do something easy, but to do something true. He came to bring truth and life" (p. 42). The truth that Christ came to reveal is the truth about Who God is, and the life that He came to give to mankind is nothing less than the life of the Holy Trinity. *No man hath seen God at any time; the Only-begotten God, Who is in the bosom of the Father, He hath declared Him* (John 1:18).

The reason Christ was persecuted by the Jewish religious leaders was because He identified Himself with God: *I and my Father are one* (John 10:30). God Himself bore witness of this at Christ's baptism in the Jordan river when a voice from heaven proclaimed: *This is My beloved Son, in Whom I am well pleased* (Matthew 3:17). Thus, Christ's life and teachings reveal that the one true God—the God of Abraham, Isaac, and Jacob—is not merely the divine Lawgiver, but first and foremost the Father, Who eternally begets His Son and breathes forth His Spirit. God is, above all else, love, as St. John the Theologian tells us.

This perfection and superabundance of love that God is cannot be contained within a single, isolated individual. True love demands the presence of another. This fact is expressed by the divine names that reveal the persons of the Godhead: Father, Son, and Spirit. These names reveal the fact that in God there is both perfect unity and oneness and genuine personal diversity. As Bishop Kallistos (Ware) puts it:

> The Christian God is not just a unit but a union, not just unity but community. There is in God something analogous to "society." He is not a single per-

THE HOLY TRINITY

son loving Himself alone, not a self-contained monad or "The One." He is triunity: three equal persons, each one dwelling in the other by virtue of an unceasing movement of mutual love (*The Orthodox Way*, p. 27).

The basic tenets of the doctrine of the Trinity may be stated rather simply, but it will take all of eternity for us to even begin to fathom the depths of the mystery of this God of Triune Love. Here, then, is a basic outline of the doctrine:

1) There is one God because there is one Father, Who is the source and principle of the Godhead. The Father begets the Son and breathes forth His Spirit. The Son is the Son *of* God, and the Spirit is the Spirit *of* God.

2) There is one and only one God. The multiplicity of persons in the Godhead in no way divides the divine unity or creates three Gods.

3) There are three co-eternal and co-equal persons in the Godhead. The absolute oneness of God in no way diminishes their personal distinctiveness and reality. In other words, the Father, Son, and Spirit are real persons, and not merely roles that the one God plays at different times.

4) In begetting the Son and breathing forth the Spirit, the Father bestows upon them the fullness of His divine being. Thus, the Father, Son, and Spirit each possess the same divine nature or essence. To describe this, the Church uses the word *consubstantial* — meaning of the same substance or nature.

5) Each person of the Godhead possesses the entirety of the divine nature. God is not divided into three parts, because the divine nature is one and indivisible. Because the Son and the Spirit possess the fullness of the divine nature, they are no less God than God the Father, even though They derive their being from Him. Each person of the Godhead is, therefore, *catholic*—meaning whole and complete.

6) Each person of the Godhead exists by the total gift of Himself to the other persons in an unbroken and perfect communion of love. The Father is the originator of this "cycle," bestowing the fullness of His being on His Son and His Spirit. They return this love to the Father and exchange it with one another, forming an unbreakable unity of love. In this way, each of the persons is said to exist in the others. It is impossible to conceive of one person without thinking of the other two persons. The Church uses the word *coinherence* (in Greek, *perichoresis*) to describe this fact.

7) This perfect communion of love is eternal. There was never a time when the Father did not beget His Son and breathe forth His Spirit. In fact, the concept of time is inapplicable to God, because it is a created phenomenon. The Holy Trinity is eternal, beyond all of our created notions of time and space. To say, then, that God begets His Son and breathes forth His Spirit does not imply temporal succession or change in God, Who is *the same yesterday, today, and forever* (Hebrews 13:8).

THE HOLY TRINITY

Although the doctrine of the Holy Trinity may seem rather abstract, it has some very practical implications for how we view reality and live our lives. First of all, the doctrine of the Trinity means that nothing that exists, whether on earth or in heaven, can be conceived of as an individual, in and of itself. God Himself is not absolute individuality, but perfect love and communion. Where there is self-contained individuality, there can be no love, for love means the total gift of oneself to another. True being is love, and where there is no love, there is only the absurdity of death and non-being. That is why Lossky said, "between the Trinity and hell there lies no other choice." Those who, in their spiritual blindness, deny the doctrine of the Trinity, deny love itself, and thus deny the truth of their own being created in the image of this God of Triune Love.

Second, the doctrine of the Trinity means that the principle and source of all that exists is not a mathematical equation, but a person. When we pray, we do not seek a state of disinterested non-being, but the personal God, Who has revealed Himself to mankind. Our salvation consists not in our learning *about* God, but in entering into a personal communion of love *with* Him: *And this is life eternal, that they might know Thee the only true God, and Jesus Christ, Whom Thou hast sent* (John 17:3).

Third, the doctrine of the Trinity means that there can be genuine diversity and even order among persons without diminishing their equality. Although the Son and the Spirit derive their being from the Father, They each possess the divine nature in its entirety and are

CHAPTER TWO

therefore equal to the Father in being. In other words, equal does not necessarily mean the same. The Father and the Son are different persons; the Father begets the Son and is the source of His being; the Son does the will of the Father; and yet They are equal in being, power, and glory. Likewise, the Spirit proceeds from the Father and rests in the Son, yet He is equal to the Father and the Son.

This, then, is the heart of the Orthodox Faith: Three unique, co-eternal, co-equal divine persons glorified in one simple and undivided Godhead.

> Come, all peoples, and let us worship the one Godhead in three persons, the Son in the Father with the Holy Spirit. For the Father gave birth outside time to the Son, co-eternal and enthroned with Him; and the Holy Spirit is glorified in the Father together with the Son: one power, one essence, one Godhead, Whom we all worship, and to Whom we say: Holy God, Who hast created all things through the Son, by the cooperation of the Holy Spirit. Holy Mighty, through Whom we know the Father, and through Whom the Holy Spirit came to dwell within the world. Holy Immortal, Paraclete Spirit, proceeding from the Father and resting on the Son. Holy Trinity, Glory to Thee (*The Pentecostarion*).

What is the meaning of life? The Holy Trinity! For without love, love which is eternal and perfect, life truly has no meaning. Into a world held captive by self-centeredness and death, Christ came to reveal the truth that God is love and to bring mankind into His eternal Trinitarian Communion:

THE HOLY TRINITY

That they all may be one; as Thou Father, art in Me, and I in Thee, that they also may be one in Us: that the world may believe that Thou has sent Me. And the glory which Thou gavest Me I have given them; that they be one, even as We are one: I in them, and Thou in Me, that they may be perfect in one; and that the world may know that Thou hast sent Me, and has loved them, as Thou hast loved Me (John 17:21-23).

THE FATHERS SPEAK

There is one and the same person of the Father, from Whom the Son is begotten, and the Holy Spirit proceeds. He is the cause of those persons who are caused by Him; and therefore we rightly assert one God, since He co-exists with them. For the persons of the Godhead are not divided from each other in time, place, will, occupation, activity, or any qualifications of this sort, the distinguishing marks observed in human beings. The only distinction here is that the Father is father, not son: the Son is son, not father; similarly the Holy Spirit is neither father nor son.

St. Gregory of Nyssa
The Later Christian Fathers
Tr. by Henry Bettenson
Oxford University Press, 1972

When the Lord taught us the doctrine of Father, Son, and Holy Spirit, He did not make arithmetic a part of this gift. . . . If we count, we do not add, increasing

CHAPTER TWO

from one to many. We do not say, "one, two, three," or "first, second, and third." God says, *I am the first and I am the last* (Revelation 1:17). We have never to this present day heard of a second God. We worship God from God, confessing the uniqueness of the persons, while maintaining the unity of the monarchy. . . . The Son is in the Father, and the Father in the Son; what the Father is, the Son is likewise, and vice-versa—such is the unity. As unique persons, They are one and one; as sharing a common nature, both are one. . . . The Holy Spirit is one, and we speak of Him as unique, since through the one Son He is joined to the Father. He completes the all-praised and blessed Trinity.

St. Basil the Great
from *On the Holy Spirit*
SVS Press, 1980

Everywhere the Apostle teaches the indivisibility and co-essentiality of the Holy Trinity, and that where the Son is, there is the Father also; and where the Father is, there is the Holy Spirit; and where the Holy Spirit is, there is the entire Godhead of three persons, the one God and Father, together with His co-essential Son and Spirit, *Who is blessed forevermore. Amen* (Romans 1:25).

St. Symeon the New Theologian
from *On the Mystical Life*
Tr. by Alexander Golitzin
SVS Press, 1996

THE HOLY TRINITY

Special Study
The Trinity in the Old Testament

Although the doctrine of the Trinity was not fully revealed until the coming of Christ, we find hints of the Trinity throughout the Old Testament of the Bible, in which is recounted the creation of the world and God's dealings with the People of Israel.

The Book of Genesis records that when God was creating mankind He said, *Let Us make man in Our image, after Our likeness* (Genesis 1:26). Our holy Fathers understood the use of the plural here as an indication of the three persons of the Trinity. The Psalmist tells us that God created the world through His Word and His Spirit: *By the Word of the LORD were the heavens made; and all the host of them by the Breath of His mouth* (Psalm 32 [33]:6†).

Furthermore, one of the Hebrew words for God, *Elohim*, carries with it the idea of plurality. Thus, the name of God itself denotes the plurality of persons within the unity of nature.

One of the most important Old Testament hints of the Trinity is the visitation of Abraham by three Angels:

---

† The numbering of the Psalms differs between the Greek and Hebrew versions of the Old Testament. The Orthodox Church follows the Greek (Septuagint) text. Almost all English translations follow the Hebrew. Here, the reference is to Psalm 32 according to the Orthodox usage. The number in brackets is the number of the Psalm in most English Bibles.

CHAPTER TWO

And the LORD *appeared unto him in the plains of Mamre: and he sat in the tent door in the heat of the day; and he lift up his eyes and looked, and, lo, three Men stood by him: and when he saw them, he ran to meet Them from the tent door, and bowed himself toward the ground, and said, "My Lord, if now I have found favor in Thy sight, pass not away, I pray Thee, from Thy servant: Let a little water, I pray You, be fetched, and wash Your feet, and rest Yourselves under the tree: and I will fetch a morsel of bread, and comfort Ye Your hearts; after that Ye shall pass on: for therefore are Ye come to Your servant." And They said, "So do, as thou hast said"* (Genesis 18:1-5).

Notice that in this account, there is a constant interplay between the singular and plural. The Lord appears to Abraham, and yet he sees three Men. He addresses Them at one point in the singular, and later in the plural. Compare this account with what St. Gregory Nazianzus (4th c.) has to say about the Trinity:

> No sooner do I conceive of the One than I am illumined by the splendor of the Three; no sooner do I distinguish them than I am carried back to the One. When I think of any One of the Three, I think of Him as the whole, and my eyes are filled, and the greater part of what I am thinking of escapes me. I cannot grasp the greatness of that One so as to attribute a greater greatness to the rest. When I contemplate the Three together, I see but one torch, and cannot divide or measure out the undivided light (*Oration* 41).

The only icon of the Trinity which the Church allows is, strictly speaking, not an icon of the Trinity per

THE HOLY TRINITY

se, but of the visitation of the three Angels to Abraham. One cannot make a pictorial representation of the Father because He is spirit and has no depictable form. Similarly, one can depict the Holy Spirit only symbolically, as a dove or as tongues of fire. The Angels, which were clearly seen by Abraham, provide the Church with an indirect way of depicting the All-holy Trinity.

The most famous icon of this kind is by the Russian iconographer St. Andrei Rublev (15th c.). Indeed, this is perhaps the most famous icon in the world. What makes this icon so special is the way in which Rublev captured the interplay between the one and the three. In the icon, we clearly see the three Angels, representing the Father, Son, and Holy Spirit. And yet, these three form a perfect circle, a complete communion of love. There is no disharmony, no rebellion or self-will among them. Rather, there is perfect concord.

One and many, motion and rest—icons of the Hospitality of Abraham capture the dynamic paradox of the Trinity and present to the faithful an image of that divine life we seek in union with the God of Triune Love. That life was revealed to the People of Israel only indirectly, in types and shadows. When Christ became man, however, the shadows passed away, and man beheld One of the Holy Trinity in the flesh. This is the essence of the Orthodox Faith.

CHAPTER TWO
Reflection

1. What word best describes the being of God?

2. Is it possible to conceive of any one person of the Holy Trinity without immediately thinking of the other two? Why?

3. Why is there one God and not three?

4. What word does the Church use to describe the unity of the nature in the Godhead?

5. What word describes the fact that each person of the Trinity possesses the entire divine nature? (Hint, we use the same word to describe the wholeness of the Church.)

6. What word does the Church use to describe the fact that each person of the Trinity lives *in* the others?

7. What Old Testament event foreshadows the revelation of the doctrine of the Trinity?

8. Are the Son and the Spirit in any way inferior to the Father?

9. Which person of the Trinity is involved in the salvation of mankind?

10. Can we consider the doctrine of the Trinity to be "optional equipment"?

Chapter Three
Creation

Man was created in the image of God in order to live in a perfect communion of love with God, with his fellow men, and with the physical world.

In the beginning God created the heaven and the earth (Genesis 1:1). So begins the Bible. It is significant that the record of God's revelation to mankind should begin in this way, for the Divine Scriptures do not simply take the existence of the world for granted. On the contrary, the Scriptures affirm that the world and all that is in it derives its being from God. The world did not create itself; it was created by God and owes its continued existence to His power and will.

The Book of Genesis, however, does not provide a scientifically detailed account of how the world was created. Rather, Genesis answers the questions Who? and Why? Genesis, therefore, is concerned with the *meaning* of the world's existence. Specifically, the Scriptures affirm two very important points about the world and about our place in it: (1) God created the world out of nothing; and (2) of all the creatures of the earth, man is unique because he is created in the image of God.

CHAPTER THREE

First of all, the world was created out of nothing (in Latin, *ex nihilo*). In the ancient world, this was a rather revolutionary idea. For the Greeks, the *cosmos* was eternal; it had no beginning and no end. They taught that God made the world out of preexistent matter. Furthermore, pagan religion affirmed that the world itself is divine (pantheism).

Against the prevailing opinions of the day, however, the divinely inspired prophets of the Old Testament and the Apostles of Christ affirmed that the world is not eternal but was created from nothing. God alone is eternal and immortal (cf. 1 Timothy 6:16). If God, as the Greek philosophers taught, had made the world out of some preexistent matter, then He would be more properly called the "arranger" of the world rather than its Creator, for the craftsman is limited by the materials with which he works. God would, then, be in some sense dependent upon matter. But such is not the case, for God created the world not because of any necessity or out of any preexistent matter, but by His free and infinite will.

Because of this, the world can in no way be considered divine. The ancient pagan religions are being revived in our own day under the guise of the New Age movement, feminist theology and witchcraft, and some extreme forms of environmentalism. Against such movements the Church firmly maintains that between the being of God and the being of the world there is an irreducible (but not irreconcilable) gulf. The world is not God. Consider the difference between the generation of the Son and the creation of the world: God eter-

CREATION

nally ("before all ages") begets His Son from His own being, while He creates the world by His will out of nothing at the beginning of time.

The fear of the LORD *is the beginning of wisdom* (Proverbs 9:10). The first step in spiritual growth is to recognize where one stands in the grand scheme of things. Man must realize that he is not his own Creator. He is not the source of his own being, and he is not self-sufficient. In other words, man is not God. This does not mean, however, that man's life has no meaning or that he is a mere "plaything" of God. On the contrary, God created man to be the crown of the entire creation and bestowed upon him an honor of infinite significance. The second major point which the Book of Genesis affirms is that man is created in the image of God to live in communion with Him throughout eternity.

The ancient philosophers took great pride in calling man a microcosm, that is, a world in miniature. But St. Gregory of Nyssa pointed out that the same could be said of a mouse. What makes man special, unique in all the created universe, is his creation in the image of God. According to Fr. George (Capsanis), Abbot of the Monastery of St. Gregory on Mt. Athos, *"Made according to the image of God signifies both the origin and goal of our existence. . . . So far as we "image forth" the wise creative God, so far do we discover in ourselves the charisms of knowledge and creativity (The Eros of Repentance,* pp. 1-2)."

But what does this mean? If man is not God, or a part of God, in what way is he created in God's image? This question admits of no simple answer, for through-

CHAPTER THREE

out history the Fathers of the Church have given many different answers. Many have said that the image of God resides in man's soul. Others have identified the image of God with man's free will, or with his ability to govern the earth. In a sense, all of these answers are correct. Perhaps it is best to say that it is the totality of man's being which constitutes the image of God. In other words, the image of God in us is everything which makes us unique personal beings.

We have already seen that God is first and foremost personal existence. He is the One for Whom "to be is to love." Thus, it is man's ability to enter into personal relationships—his ability to love—that makes him a being like unto God. Man is, in other words, created in the image of the Holy Trinity. For man to be what he was created to be, to fulfill his cosmic destiny, he must attain unto the likeness of the Father and the Son and the Holy Spirit.

Man is, therefore, an inherently relational being; he cannot be conceived of as an "individual." In the words of the English clergyman and poet, John Donne, "No man is an island entire of himself." For man, to be is to be in relation to others. Specifically, this means that man is created to relate to God, to his fellow men, and to the physical world.

More than anything else, man is created to be in a relationship of love with the God Who made him. St. Athanasius the Great wrote, "For of what use is existence to the creature if it cannot know its Maker?" Truly man's sojourn on earth would be pointless if he had no way of knowing and loving the One Who gave him

CREATION

being. God did not create man as a robot or a pet. Out of His infinite love and wisdom He bestowed upon man the capacity to know and love his Maker as Friend and Father. This is the center of man's being, the purpose for which he was created. Without this loving relationship with God, man is not fully human—he is but an empty shell, destined to return to the earth from which he was made. As Blessed Augustine said, "Our hearts can have no rest until they rest in Thee."

Secondly, man is created to be in a relationship of love with his fellow men. God said, *It is not good that man should be alone* (Genesis 2:18). With these words, God ruled out the possibility that man was created to be an isolated individual, a prisoner of his own ego. Just as the Father, Son, and Spirit dwell together in an unbreakable communion of love, so man, created in the image of the Holy Trinity, is meant to dwell in unity and harmony with his fellow men. *Behold, how good and pleasant it is for brethren to dwell together in unity* (Psalm 132[133]:1).

For man to be what he is created to be, he must love all people, *for love is of God; and everyone that loveth is born of God and knoweth God* (1 John 4:7). Thus also our Lord enjoins us: *This is My commandment, that ye love one another, as I have loved you* (John 15:12). Every rationalistic philosophy, every form of "humanism," that exalts the individual and considers him to be the absolute value in life is an unholy caricature of true human life and leads man only to hell. St. Maximus the Confessor (6th-7th c.) sums up the matter quite succinctly: "Do not disdain the commandment of love, because by it you will be a son of God. If you transgress it you will become a son of hell."

Finally, man is created to be in a relationship of love with the physical world. This is not to say that man is to love the world as an end in itself, but that the world is to become a part of his loving relationship with God. And God said, *"Let Us make man in Our image, after Our likeness: and let them have dominion over the fish of the sea, and over the fowl of the air, and over the cattle, and over all the earth, and over every creeping thing that creepeth upon the earth"* (Genesis 1:26).

Man was created last, as the crown and glory of the whole creation. The world was created for man, so that through his wise and loving use of it, it might be a means of communion with God. This does not mean that man has a right to abuse the world and treat it as a disposable commodity, but it does mean that the world was created to be man's servant. The proper relationship of man to the world is a sacramental one: man is to receive the world as God's gift and offer it back to God, along with his whole life, in a sacrifice of love and obedience.

Man's creation in the image of the Holy Trinity means that man's very being and the way he is to live out his life is designed to image forth the life of God Himself. In this way, man attains unto the likeness of God. Just as the eternal Son of God—the perfect Image of the Father—receives His being from the Father and offers all that He is back to the Father in love, so man, created in the image of God, is meant to offer all that he is back to God in love.

CREATION

In this way, man's being is established in the eternal and perfect love of God. This is what truly defines man's being and gives purpose to his life. As we read in the Book of Genesis, however, and as we know from personal experience, man has rejected his God-created vocation of communion with the All-Holy Trinity and has thus failed to achieve the purpose for which he was created. This is known as the "Fall" or the "Original Sin." We shall address this failure in the next chapter, but, for now, let us consider the great glory for which we were created and the true value of our lives as persons created in the image of God:

> [Man] was deemed worthy by God of such honor and providential care that before him this entire sensible world came into being for his sake, and before him right from the foundation of the world the kingdom of heaven was prepared for his sake, and counsel concerning him was taken beforehand, and he was formed by the hand of God and according to the image of God (St. Gregory Palamas, *One Hundred and Fifty Chapters*).

CHAPTER THREE
THE FATHERS SPEAK

Grudging existence to none, therefore, He [God] made all things out of nothing through His own Word, our Lord Jesus Christ; and of all these His earthly creatures He reserved especial mercy for the race of men. Upon them, therefore, upon men who, as animals, were essentially impermanent, He bestowed a grace which other creatures lacked—namely, the impress of His own image, a share in the reasonable being of the very Word Himself, so that, reflecting Him and themselves becoming reasonable and expressing the Mind of God even as He does, though in limited degree, they might continue forever in the blessed and only true life of the Saints in Paradise.

St. Athanasius the Great
from *On the Incarnation*
SVS Press, 1982

In this manner, then, it is demonstrated that there is one God, the Father uncreated, invisible, Creator of all things, above Whom there is no other God and after Whom there is no other God (cf. Isaiah 43:10). God is rational, and therefore made His creation by His Word. He is also spirit, so He fashioned all things by His Spirit. As the prophet puts it, *By the Word of the Lord the heavens were established, and all the power of them by His Spirit* (Psalm 32[33]:6). The Word establishes and gives body and substance, while the Spirit gives order and form to the various powers.

St. Irenaios of Lyons
from *The Preaching of the Apostles*

CREATION

Special Study
Creation and Evolution

American society as a whole, and certainly the authors of science textbooks, simply assume evolution to be a scientifically established fact. Those who do not accept this assumption are labeled as "fundamentalists," "obscurantists," and "intellectual cave men." It is not surprising, therefore, that many religious thinkers, including a few Orthodox Christians, have accepted the evolutionary worldview and have tried to reconcile it with the biblical doctrine of creation.

Before we proceed any further, let us define exactly what is meant by evolution. I am not referring to the natural process whereby the characteristics of species are changed and adapted to their environments (*micro* evolution). I am, rather, referring to the theory according to which *all* life on earth evolved in a completely *random* process from the *chance self-creation* of living cells from a "pre-biotic soup" of elements at the dawn of the earth's history (*macro* evolution).

Evolution is a materialistic *philosophy* which seeks to explain the world *solely* in terms of itself, without *any* reference to a Creator. It should be obvious, therefore, that evolution is incompatible with the Orthodox worldview. Indeed, in the words of Fr. Seraphim Rose,

CHAPTER THREE

"It's a *rival thought-pattern* to Orthodoxy, not just another idea" (*Not of this World*, p. 512).

But how can the Church disagree with scientific fact? Is this not the same as believing that the earth is flat or that it is the center of the solar system? Furthermore, could not God have used evolution to bring about the creation of man?

Theistic evolution, or the belief that God created and directs the evolutionary process, would be a plausible philosophy *if* there were any real, scientific proof of evolution. However, there is none. To be sure, there is ample proof of species changing and adapting to their environments, but no proof whatsoever that one classification of animal evolved into another classification.

Although literally hundreds of thousands of fossils have been discovered in the last 135 years, the same gaps in the fossil record remain today that so troubled Charles Darwin when he wrote *The Origin of Species*. The novel evolutionary theory known as Punctuated Equilibrium, put forth by Harvard paleontologist Stephen Jay Gould, is nothing more than an admission that the gaps in the fossil record are real and will not be filled in. In other words, there are no missing links.

Furthermore, the development of molecular biology has shown that living cells are far more complex than Darwin or anyone in the nineteenth century had imagined. The simplest living cell is a far more complicated machine than any human invention. In order to successfully duplicate itself, it must contain exactly the right acids and enzymes, each in is proper place, performing its assigned function, processing literally millions of pieces of information. Statistically, the chances of such a cell coming into being as a result of the random conglomeration of acids are astronomically remote. No molecular biologist has been able to come up with a plausible explanation for the emergence of necessary cell components such as DNA, much less for the emergence of living cells themselves.

If evolution has never actually been proven, why is it universally accepted as an established fact? The answer is quite simple. Modern science assumes that the world is explainable solely in terms of itself. Scientists may not be able to explain how random amino acids accidentally formed cells or how amphibians evolved into mammals, but they have no other choice but to accept the "truth" of evolution as long as they assume that world explains itself. In other words, evolution *must* be true, because modern, scientific method *needs* it to be true.

It should be noted that this line of reasoning is not only circular, it is inherently religious. The *a priori* assumption that the world is explainable solely in terms of itself is itself not based upon empirical investigation. In 1993, noted evolutionist and philosopher of science Michael Ruse admitted as much before a scientific convocation called to debunk creationism. This admission came ten years after he had testified in an Arkansas court that evolution was *not* based on any preconceived philosophical notions.

The acceptance of evolution as fact has grave ramifications for human society. If man is nothing more than

CHAPTER THREE

an evolved animal, then there is no *rational* basis for asserting the inherent dignity of man.

"Social Darwinism" was an attempt initiated by Darwin's own cousin to apply the principles of natural selection and survival of the fittest to human society. Although it is common for evolutionists to disavow *any* relation with Social Darwinism, Darwin's own writings make it clear that he was sympathetic to the idea. Indeed, Social Darwinism is a perfectly *logical* extension of the theory of evolution.

The "science" of eugenics was born out of this movement. Eugenics was (and is) an attempt to create better humans through scientific methods of population control and selective breeding. Widely practiced in Great Britain and the United States in the early part of this century, eugenics became the "scientific" basis for Hitler's attempt to create a Master Race. Hitler's initial attempts at population control (the forced sterilization of the mentally retarded) and selective breeding (laws regulating mixed marriages) were based on existing laws in force in Britain and the U.S. These programs ultimately led to extermination camps for "undesirables" and to breeding camps for pure-blooded Germans.

Fifty years after the end of World War II, little has changed except for the sophistication of the methods. Abortion as population control, genetic engineering, and designer sperm banks are all the result of a materialistic worldview, which assumes that man is nothing more than an evolved animal. Why then, should man not try to "improve" himself by altering his genetic makeup? Why, indeed, should one assume that all men are equal?

The Orthodox doctrine of creation is wholly incompatible with such an approach. It is an unalterable dogma of the Orthodox Church that each and every human being, from the moment of conception, is a unique and unrepeatable person created in the image of God. Furthermore, because man is created in the image of the Holy Trinity, human nature itself is one and indivisible. Each human being possesses and sums up in himself the entirety of human nature. Therefore, all men are equal, regardless of their race, mental capacities, or situation in life.

The theory of evolution is not simply a matter for scientists. It has a direct effect on how we view the world and man's place in it. Therefore, it is incumbent upon all Orthodox Christians to clearly understand the issues involved. For a popular discussion of evolution see Philip Johnson's *Darwin on Trial* (InterVarsity Press, 1991). For more detailed treatments, written by professional scientists, see Michael Denton's *Evolution: A Theory in Crisis* (Adler and Adler, 1986) and *Darwin's Black Box: The Biochemical Challenge to Evolution* (Free Press, 1996) by Michael Behe.

CHAPTER THREE

Reflection

1. From what did God create the world?

2. Did God have to create the world?

3. What separates man from the rest of creation?

4. In what way is man created in the image of God?

5. What does it mean that man is a "relational" being?

6. In what way does man's relationship with God reflect the Son's eternal relationship with the Father?

7. Can man be defined as a "rugged individual"?

8. How is man's relationship with his fellow men related to his creation in the image of God?

9. What is the biblical basis for the equality of the human race?

10. How is man's use of the physical world related to his creation in the image of God?

Chapter Four
The Fall of Mankind

Through his disobedience man has rejected his divine vocation and has failed to realize his life as love and communion with the All-holy Trinity.

God created man in His own image so that through the use of his free will, in returning all that God had given him in an offering of love, man might grow ever more like God in an eternal communion of love with the Father, the Son, and the Holy Spirit. Only in this way could man fulfill the destiny for which he was created; only in this way could man become truly human. As Fr. Dimitru Staniloae said, "The glory to which man is called is that he should grow more godlike by growing ever more human."

Because this relationship of love presupposes man's free gift of himself, his creation in the image of God entailed the possibility that man would not return God's love and therefore fail to fulfill his divine calling. Indeed, this is what happened. In the Book of Genesis we read that the first-formed man—Adam, which means "man"—disobeyed God and was expelled from Paradise. This event is known as the "Fall" and the "Original Sin." Every human being, without exception, is

CHAPTER FOUR

scarred by the effects of the Fall, for the unity of human nature is such that the sin of one effects the lives of all.

The story itself is cast in very simple terms. God gave all the plants and trees in the world for man's nourishment and use except for one: the tree of the knowledge of good and evil. The serpent appeared to the first woman—Eve, which means "mother of all the living"—and enticed her to eat the forbidden fruit so that she might become like God. Eve then gave the fruit to Adam, who followed suit. For this transgression, man was barred from Paradise and doomed to return to the dust from which he was taken: *for dust thou art, and unto dust shalt thou return* (Genesis 3:19).

The Fall of mankind, however, is much more complicated than a simple act of disobedience. Man's act was ultimately a refusal to love, a refusal to enter into communion with the God Who had created him. God gave the world to mankind not merely as a source of biological sustenance, but as communion with Himself. In his book, *For the Life of the World,* Father Alexander Schmemann described God's gift in this way:

> All that exists is God's gift to man, and it all exists to make God known to man, to make man's life communion with God. It is divine love made food, made life for man. God blesses everything He creates, and, in biblical language, this means that He makes all creation the sign and means of His presence and wisdom, love and revelation (p. 14).

Mankind's proper response to this gift of love—the only possible human response—is to receive this gift of

THE FALL OF MANKIND

"divine love made food" with thanksgiving and offer it back to God in love.

There was one tree in the Garden, however, which God did not bless and did not give to man as communion with Himself. The serpent tempted Eve with the suggestion: *Ye shall not surely die: for God doth know that in the day ye eat thereof, then your eyes shall be opened, and ye shall be as gods, knowing good and evil* (Genesis 3:4-5). This was Satan's great lie to mankind: that by eating of this tree man would become like God.

God, our all-loving Creator, did not begrudge anything to mankind, even likeness unto Himself. Indeed, this was the purpose for which man was created: to become like God. But this is only possible through communion with Him, for He is love and communion. Man, however, chose to deify himself by eating of the one tree that was not given to him for communion with God. In other words, man tried to become like God without God! Fr. Schmemann wrote, the tree "is the image of the world loved for itself, and eating it is the image of life understood as an end in itself" (*For the Life of the World,* p. 16).

This "simple" act of disobedience on the part of Adam and Eve, therefore, is one of cosmic significance, for it is mankind's "no, thank you" to God. It is man's refusal to realize his life as love and communion with the God Who made him. As a result, man has made his life and the world in which he lives into a closed circuit. Instead of offering his life to God in a sacrifice of love, man has chosen to treat the world as an end in and of itself. In doing so, he has cut himself off from the only

CHAPTER FOUR

source of life and everlasting happiness. No longer is the world a source of communion with God; it has become solely a means of biological sustenance.

For in the day that thou eatest thereof thou shalt surely die (Genesis 2:17). The inevitable result of man's free choice not to respond to God in love is death. But this death is not merely the cessation of biological life. Adam and Eve continued to live "biologically" after their transgression and expulsion from Paradise. They lived out the normal course of their physical lives, but the life they lived was a living death. They had died to God, and this death made their biological deaths the permanent end to a pointless life. Created to live eternally in communion with the God Who is love, man has enslaved himself to the limitations of his biological existence. *Who,* said St. Paul, *shall deliver me from this body of death* (Romans 7:25)?

Because man's life is no longer oriented toward fulfilling his destiny in the image of God, all of his personal attributes and capacities have become misdirected. Normal energies and desires are transformed into passions that rule man's life. No longer eating in order to live, man lives in order to eat and satisfy the desires over which he has lost control. As St. Paul said, *For that which I do I allow not: for what I would, that do I not, but what I hate, that do I* (Romans 7:15). Enslaved to his bodily needs and desires, and above all enslaved to the inevitability of death, man has made of his life an ugly caricature of the life for which he was created.

By alienating himself from God, the source of love and life, man has also alienated himself from his fellow

THE FALL OF MANKIND

men and from the world in which he lives. As an isolated, self-centered ego, enslaved by his passions and the need to survive, man sees other people as objects to be used to attain his own desires or as threats to his individuality and "freedom." Every ligament of our society is torn by man's self-centeredness and greed. Nations war against each other over a few square miles of earth, and ethnic groups war against other ethnic groups for reasons too ancient for anyone living to recall. Even the most primary social unit—the family—is engulfed in infidelity, bitterness, possessiveness, and hatred.

"Hell," said the French existentialist philosopher Sartre, "is other people." But Dostoyevsky, the great, Russian Orthodox novelist of the nineteenth century, came much closer to the truth when he observed that hell is "the suffering of being no longer able to love." Indeed, the problem of man lies within the depths of his own being: having cut himself off from communion with the God of love, man has rendered himself unable to truly love his fellow men. This is the nature of man's Fall; this is the beginning of his hell.

The effects of man's Fall, however, are not limited to his relationship with other people. Indeed the whole created order—including the physical world—bears the marks of man's refusal to love. *For we know that the whole creation groaneth and travaileth in pain together until now* (Romans 8:22). The world has become a disposable commodity. Meant to be a means of communion with God, the world is now no more than an object for the fulfillment of man's self-centered desires.

CHAPTER FOUR

Thus, the Fall has blinded man's spiritual eyes. He is no longer able to see God in the world, but sees the world and his life in it as an end in itself. The life of this world is the only life which man now knows; it has become the sum total of his existence. But this world was created from nothing and exists by the good will of its Creator; it has no life of its own. Apart from God, this world and man's life in it is a "tale told by an idiot, full of sound and fury, signifying nothing" (*Macbeth*). As Fr. Schmemann said,

> The world of nature, cut off from the source of life, is a dying world. For one who thinks food in itself is the source of life, eating is communion with the dying world, it is communion with death. Food itself is dead, it is life that has died and it must be kept in refrigerators like a corpse (*For the Life of the World*, p. 17).

Many so-called Christians today have relegated the story of Adam and Eve to the realm of religious "mythology." It is a quaint story, so they say, that may help us to understand how the ancient Israelites regarded the state of man. But it can have no real bearing on how we as modern, scientifically minded people view the world and our place within it. Ironically, the arrogance of such a statement testifies to its utter falsehood, for it is the curse of fallen man that he deludes himself into taking the fallen state of things as normal. While it is certainly true that the Genesis account is not "history," in the modern sense of the word, neither is it simply a "story" or a religious "myth." The Fall of man is the most real fact of man's life, whether he realizes it

THE FALL OF MANKIND

or not. A quick glance at this morning's newspaper will easily confirm this.

The Good News, however, is that this sorry estate of man is not the end of the story. Even as God was expelling Adam and Eve from Paradise, He promised to rectify the mess man had made of his life and redeem the wayward creatures made in His image. Through the seed of Eve, God would enter into human history and once again enable man to know Him and participate in His unending life. Thus, even in the midst of the tragedy of man's Fall, the God Who is infinite love has not given up on us but desires that *all be saved and come unto the knowledge of the truth* (1 Timothy 2:4).

THE FATHERS SPEAK

For God had made man thus (that is, an embodied spirit), and had willed that he should remain in incorruption. But men, having turned from the contemplation of God to evil of their own devising, had come inevitably under the law of death. Instead of remaining in the state in which God had created them, they were in process of becoming corrupted entirely, and death had them completely under its dominion . . . and as they had at the beginning come into being out of non-existence, so were they now on the way to returning, through corruption, to non-existence again. The presence and love of the Word had called them into being; inevitably, therefore, when they lost the knowledge of

CHAPTER FOUR

God, they lost existence with it; for it is God alone Who exists, evil is non-being, the negation and antithesis of good.

St. Athanasius the Great
from *On the Incarnation*

The soul of Adam fell sick when he was exiled from Paradise, and many were the tears he shed in his distress. Likewise every soul that has known the Lord yearns for Him and cries: "Where art Thou, O Lord? Where art Thou, my Light? What hinders Him from dwelling in me? This hinders Him: Christ-like humility and love for my enemies are not in me."

St. Silouan of Mt. Athos
from *Wisdom from Mt. Athos*
Tr. by Rosemary Edmonds
St. Vladimir's Press, 1974

Light does not fail because men have blinded themselves; it remains, with its own properties, while the blinded are plunged in darkness through their own fault. . . . Therefore, all who revolt from the Father's light, and who transgress the law of liberty, have removed themselves through their own fault, since they were created free and self-determining.

St. Irenaios of Lyons
from *Against Heresies*
The Early Christian Fathers
Tr. by Henry Bettenson
Oxford University Press, 1969

THE FALL OF MANKIND
Special Study
The Passions

Human nature possesses various faculties and energies which are essential to its makeup. The Fathers, following an observation first made by Plato, frequently classify these faculties as three powers: the intelligent, the appetitive, and the irascible. The intelligent power refers to man's ability to reason. The appetitive power refers to man's desire, whether for food, or happiness, or sexual fulfillment. Man's irascible power refers to his ability to get angry or feel vehemently.

Bishop Hierotheos (Vlachos) underscores the fact that these are all quite *natural* energies which become sinful passions only when they are misdirected:

> These three powers of the soul must be turned towards God. However, when they turn against God and against our brothers instead, we have the development of passions. So a passion is a movement of the soul contrary to nature (*The Illness and Cure of the Soul in the Orthodox Tradition,* p. 137).

Let us begin by considering man's rational faculty. St. Maximus the Confessor described the proper function of this energy of the soul: "It is according to nature that the rational element in us be subjected to the divine Word and that it govern our irrational element." The Greek word for the intelligent or rational aspect of the soul is an adjectival form of the word *logos*. Man's *logos*,

CHAPTER FOUR

therefore, has a natural affinity with the *Logos* (Word) of God, Who created it.

Notice that man's rational faculty is designed to govern all of man's other faculties. When man's intelligence is subjected to the Word of God, it functions properly and is able to govern all aspects of human life. When, on the other hand, the intellect turns away from the knowledge of God, it becomes susceptible to ignorance and folly, giving itself over to fantasies and wild imaginations. In such a state, it is unable to govern the rest of man's faculties.

Just as man's rational faculty has the Word of God as its natural focus, so also man's appetitive faculty has God as its natural aim. Fr. Alexander Schmemann wrote, "Man is a hungry being. But he is hungry for God. Behind all the hunger of our life is God. All desire is finally a desire for him" (*For the Life of the World*, p. 14).

The various eating disorders discussed in popular magazines and afternoon talk shows are all examples of man's natural desire for food turned perverse. Gluttony and all of the other appetitive passions are physical manifestations of a *spiritual* disorder. All are rooted in man's Fall away from God and his failure to seek God alone as his ultimate joy.

The irascible power is also a natural faculty of the human makeup, which was given to man that he might turn away from evil. St. Isaiah the Solitary said, "Without anger a man cannot attain purity: he has to feel angry with all that is sown in him by the enemy" (*The Philokalia*, vol. 1).

THE FALL OF MANKIND

Because of self-centeredness, however, man has turned his anger away from its proper aim—the devil—towards his fellow men. When we do not get our way, when we are unable to fulfill the inordinate desires which have come to rule our life, we become angry, and life becomes bitter.

To understand more clearly how the passions govern our life, let us consider cigarette smoking. Millions of Americans continue to smoke, and millions more take up the habit even though it has been scientifically demonstrated that smoking is highly injurious to one's health. Why? First of all because they find smoking pleasurable, and secondly because nicotine is addictive.

Notice that in the case of the smoker, the desire for the pleasure of smoking overrules the intelligence. He smokes even though he knows it is bad for him. Once addicted, the smoker *must* have a cigarette or he becomes irritable. The rational faculty of the soul is unable to govern the appetitive, and when the appetitive cannot be satisfied, the irascible faculty begins to dominate man's life.

All of us, to one degree or another, are caught up in the same snare as the smoker. We have all inherited a nature in which our natural energies are easily misdirected and subjugated to evil. To rectify this situation and restore our faculties to their proper function is well beyond our power. Only God, Who created us and loves us, can restore human nature to its original glory and purpose.

CHAPTER FOUR

Reflection

1. Why was the world given to mankind?

2. Was it a sin for Adam and Eve to want to be like God?

3. What is the true nature of the "Original Sin"?

4. What is the inevitable result of man's loss of communion with God?

5. What happens to man's natural faculties and energies when his life is not directed toward its proper aim?

6. What does the Church usually call these misdirected energies?

7. How has the Fall affected man's relationship with his fellow men?

8. Should we view hell more as a special "place of punishment" or as the natural consequence of man's sin?

9. How is the Fall of man reflected in his (mis)use of the natural world?

10. Has God allowed the Fall of man to be the final chapter in human history?

Chapter Five

The Promised Messiah of Israel

God chose the descendants of Abraham—the People of Israel—to prepare the world for the coming of Christ, Who is the Messiah of Israel and the Savior of the world.

When God expelled Adam and Eve from Paradise, He made clear to them the consequences of their sin. And yet, in the midst of what was an otherwise bleak day for mankind, God made a promise which held out the hope for the future redemption and salvation of the human race. Speaking to the serpent who had deceived Eve, God said, *And I will put enmity between thee and the woman, and between thy seed and her seed; It shall bruise thy head, and thou shalt bruise His heel* (Genesis 3:15). Here we have the first indication that God was not about to let sin and death have the last word. He promised that one day the seed of Eve, though Himself bruised by the attacks of the devil, would crush the head of the serpent and forever destroy the dominion of sin and death, which holds mankind in its sway.

This, however, did not happen overnight. Mankind at this point was not yet ready to receive its Savior. The

CHAPTER FIVE

way had to be prepared. Man's mind and heart—darkened by sin and self-centeredness—had to be "trained" to hear once again the Word of God and recognize His presence in the world. It was not until this was accomplished, at *the fullness of time* (Galatians 4:4), that God send forth His Only-begotten Son into the world to become man for us.

This task of preparation began with a man named Abram:

> *Now the* LORD *had said unto Abram, "Get thee out of thy country, and from thy kindred, and from thy father's house, unto a land that I will show thee: and I will make of thee a great nation, and I will bless thee, and make thy name great; and thou shalt be a blessing: and I will bless them that bless thee, and curse him that curseth thee: and in thee shall all families of the earth be blessed"* (Genesis 12:1-3).

According to the promise of God, Abram—whose name was changed to Abraham—became the father of a great nation, that is, the People of Israel. Through this nation God would prepare the world for the coming of His Son, and, in this way, all the peoples of the world—not just the Jews—would be blessed by God.

When Abraham's descendants were being held in slavery in Egypt, God raised up Moses to deliver the People of God and lead them into the land that God had promised to their forefathers. The night before the Israelites were freed, the Angel of Death passed over the land of Egypt and slew the first born males of both man and beast. Only the Israelites, who had slain a lamb and spread its blood on their doorposts, escaped

THE PROMISED MESSIAH OF ISRAEL

this judgment of God. This event became known as the Exodus, and it is commemorated every year by the Jews at the Feast of Passover (cf. Exodus 11:4—12:20). There is much more, however, to this event than the deliverance of Israel from bondage to the Egyptians. This event is also a type or a foreshadowing of the deliverance which Christ would one day bring to all mankind. Christ Himself is our Paschal (Passover) Lamb, slain for the salvation of the world (1 Corinthians 5:7). By His Blood, we all are delivered from the bondage of sin, corruption, and death.

Having brought the People of Israel out of Egypt and across the Red Sea, Moses led them to Mt. Sinai, where he received from God the Ten Commandments and instructions for proper worship. Through the Law (*Torah*), Israel came to know the true God and learned how men ought to live with one another.

The basic "creed" of Israel is known as the *Shema*: *Hear, O Israel: The LORD our God is one LORD* (Deuteronomy 6:4). Most ancient peoples—and not a few modern ones—were polytheistic. That is, they believed in a multitude of gods. Israel, however, was taught that there was one and only one God. Furthermore, she was taught that this one God was the Creator of heaven and earth.

You will recall that the source of all of man's trouble was his attempt to make himself into God apart from the only true and living God. In the Law of Moses, however, God made it perfectly clear that He alone is God and that He will admit no rivals. The first of the Ten Commandments states, *I am the Lord thy God, Who*

CHAPTER FIVE

have brought thee out of the land of Egypt, out of the house of bondage. Thou shalt have no other gods before Me (Exodus 20:2).

Thus, in electing Israel as His own people, God brought her to the knowledge of Himself. It was His desire that she learn to do His will in all things, so that one day Israel might bring forth her most perfect fruit: the one who in perfect love and purity of heart would surrender her whole being to God and become a vessel worthy to bear the Son of God in the flesh. The Most Blessed Virgin Mary is, therefore, the final and consummate act in God's program of preparation. From her inviolate womb comes forth the Messiah of Israel — the One Who, in His flesh, is the fulfillment of all the promises of God to Israel and to the world.

Everything which happened to the People of Israel was a preparation for Christ. Everything points to His coming and to His work of salvation. Specifically, however, there are three offices which are singled out in particular as being "Messianic," that is, offices which specifically point to the person and work of Christ: prophet, priest, and king.

The first of these offices is that of prophet. Unfortunately, many people equate prophecy with fortune-telling. The word, however, actually means to "speak forth." It means to declare the truth of the Lord. Thus, when the prophets spoke to Israel, they were not engaging in a carnival sideshow but were proclaiming the message of God's love and salvation. This was true even when they were rebuking the People of Israel for their sins and faithlessness. When the prophets attacked the hypocrisy of Israel, they were trying to reveal the inner essence of the Law. That inner essence and meaning is none other than Christ Himself, the Son of God. It is Christ, the eternal Word and Wisdom of the Father, Who is the purpose and content of the Law of Moses.

However, the prophets point to Christ not only by announcing prophecies concerning Him (cf. Isaiah 7:14), but by simply being prophets—people who proclaim the Word of God. By proclaiming the Word of God in their time, they pointed to the Word of God Himself, Who would become man and reveal God to mankind in the most perfect way. *God, Who at sundry times and in divers manners spake in time past unto the fathers by the prophets, hath in these last days spoken unto us by His Son, Whom He hath appointed heir of all things, by Whom also He made the worlds* (Hebrews 1:1-2).

The second "Messianic Office" is that of priest. When God gave the Law to Moses, He also gave him specific instructions for proper worship, including instructions for the priesthood. The most important function of the priest was to make sacrifices on behalf of the people. Once a year the high priest entered into the Holy of Holies to make the sacrifice for the sins of Israel (cf. Leviticus 16:15-16).

These sacrifices, however, had to be repeated, for they were unable to heal the great wound caused by sin and raise mankind up again unto the likeness of its heavenly archetype. Their purpose was to point to the One Who is both perfect Priest and Sacrifice:

CHAPTER FIVE

For the Law having a shadow of good things to come, and not the very image of the things, can never with those sacrifices which they offered year by year continually make the comers thereunto perfect. For then would they not have ceased to be offered? Because that the worshippers once purged should have had no more conscience of sins. But in those sacrifices there is a remembrance again made of sins every year. For it is not possible that the blood of bulls and of goats should take away sins. Wherefore when He cometh into the world, He saith, sacrifice and offering Thou wouldest not, but a body hast Thou prepared Me: In burnt offerings and sacrifices for sin Thou hast had no pleasure. Then said I, Lo, I come (in the volume of the book it is written of Me,) to do Thy will, O God. Above when He said, sacrifice and offering and burnt offerings and offering for sin Thou wouldest not, neither hadst pleasure therein; which are offered by the Law; Then said He, Lo, I come to do Thy will, O God. He taketh away the first, that He may establish the second. By the which will we are sanctified through the offering of the Body of Jesus Christ once for all (Hebrews 10:1-10).

The third "Messianic Office" is that of king. Originally Israel did not have a king, or rather, she had God for her sovereign. But, in an effort to "keep up with the Joneses" (cf. 1 Samuel 8:5), Israel insisted on having a king. Her first king, Saul, turned out to be a tyrant, but his successor, David, was a man after God's own heart. Although David was certainly not perfect, his kingship became a type of the kingship of Christ. Indeed, Jesus' human lineage is traced from David. The New Testament begins with the words, *The book of the generation of*

THE PROMISED MESSIAH OF ISRAEL

Jesus Christ, the son of David, the son of Abraham (Matthew 1:1).

David is the author of many of the hymns contained in the Book of Psalms. Many of these psalms refer not only to David, but to the Messiah Who would sit on David's throne:

> *Why do the heathen rage, and the people imagine a vain thing? The kings of the earth set themselves, and the rulers take counsel together, against the* LORD, *and against His Anointed[†] , saying, Let us break their bands asunder, and cast away their cords from us. He that sitteth in the heavens shall laugh: the Lord shall have them in derision. Then shall He speak unto them in His wrath, and vex them in his sore displeasure. Yet have I set My king upon My holy hill of Zion. I will declare the decree: the* LORD *hath said unto Me, Thou art My Son; this day have I begotten Thee.* (Psalm 2:1-7)

Every aspect of the life of the People of Israel points beyond itself to Christ. Apart from Him, Israel is just an ancient culture alongside other ancient cultures. What makes Israel special is the fact that she existed not for her own sake, but for the sake of God and His Christ. In doing so, Israel existed for the sake of the whole world, for every people and land. Through the descendent of Abraham, a son of the tribe of Judah (David's tribe), every nation of the world has been blessed.

[†] Christ is Greek for "Anointed One" or "Messiah."

CHAPTER FIVE

THE FATHERS SPEAK

The lyre of the prophets who proclaimed Him, singing before Him, and the hyssop of the priests who loved Him, eagerly desiring His presence, and the diadem of kings who handed it down in succession belong to this Lord of virgins, for even His mother is a virgin. He Who is King gives the kingdom to all. He Who is Priest gives pardon to all. He Who is the Lamb gives nourishment to all.

Let His mother worship Him; let her offer Him a crown. For Solomon's mother made him king and crowned him. He apostatized and lost his crown in battle. Behold the Son of David Who glorified and crowned the House of David! For You have greatly magnified his throne, and You have greatly exalted his tribe, and his lyre You have extended everywhere.

> **St. Ephrem the Syrian**
> from *Hymns on the Nativity*
> Tr. by Kathleen McVey
> Paulist Press, 1989

Even though in Scripture there were many righteous men and friends of God before the coming of the Justifier and Reconciler, we ought to consider this both in the particular context of their own generation and also with reference to that which was to come. It was for this that they were enabled and prepared . . . that when the light would shine they would see it, and when the reality had been disclosed they would rise above the types and shadows.

> **St. Nicholas Cabasilas**
> from *The Life in Christ*
> Tr. by C. J. deCatanzaro
> SVS Press, 1974

THE PROMISED MESSIAH OF ISRAEL
Special Study
Typology

We have spoken of certain Old Testament persons or events as being *types* of something revealed in the New Testament. We saw that the three Angels who visited Abraham were a type of the Holy Trinity. We also noted that the Exodus of the Jews from Egypt was a type of the deliverance of mankind from sin by the Blood of Christ. But what exactly is a type, and why does the Church interpret the Scriptures in this way?

Typology is a method of biblical interpretation whereby certain persons or events (usually in the Old Testament) are seen as signs or foreshadowings of either heavenly realities or future events. This method of interpretation was employed by Christ Himself when He cited Jonah's three-day sojourn in the belly of the great fish as a sign of His own three-day burial (Matthew 12:39-40). In the book of Hebrews, the priest Melchizedek, to whom Abraham offered a tenth of his goods (Genesis 14:18-20), is cited as a type of Christ, the great High Priest of our salvation (Hebrews 6:20ff.).

Typology is very similar to the literary technique of foreshadowing. Let us suppose that the author of a novel has his main character die in the final chapter by being hit by a car on a deserted, country road. Let us also suppose that in an earlier chapter, the main character comes upon a dead animal, obviously hit by a car, on a deserted, country road, and that in order to avoid

CHAPTER FIVE

the animal he swerves off the road and damages his car. Because of this minor accident he misses an important meeting, and the course of his life is altered.

The dead animal in the road has a specific function in the development of the plot up to that point. We might have no reason to suspect that the animal carcass has any other meaning. When, however, we read the last chapter and learn that the main character is killed by being hit by a car on a deserted, country road, we think back to the dead animal in the earlier chapter.

The author could have used any excuse to keep the main character from getting to his meeting. His car could have simply broken down. He could have had a minor accident with another car at a busy intersection, or he could have swerved to miss a large tree limb in the middle of the road. Instead, the author chose to foreshadow the death of the main character by using an animal that also had been hit by a car.

While the actual text of the Bible was written by men, the true author of the story is God Himself. Indeed, He is both the author and the main character. Throughout the history of Israel, God was preparing Israel and the world for the coming of His Son. When the Son was finally revealed in human flesh, the eternal significance of the history of Israel came to light.

The Jews whom Moses led out of Egypt had no indication that their Exodus meant anything more than their escape from physical bondage. However, its *real* significance was not understood until the coming of Christ, Who delivered all mankind from the bondage of sin and death through the shedding of His own Blood.

THE PROMISED MESSIAH OF ISRAEL

The Church interprets *all* of the Holy Scripture, both Old and New Testaments, in the light of Christ, and typology is the primary method used. Two points need to be clarified, however.

First, because God is both author and main character, the types do more than simply foreshadow; in some way they actually *participate* in the event being typified. Thus, when Abraham encountered the three Angels, he was actually encountering, in a limited way, the Holy Trinity. When Israel escaped from Egypt, she was participating, again in a very limited way, in the deliverance of Christ.

Finally, we must understand that typology is different from allegory. Allegory is a method of interpretation, also used by the Apostles and Church Fathers, whereby a moral or philosophical point is extracted from a story, without regard to its literal meaning. These two types of interpretation are not mutually exclusive. The Fathers teach us that a passage may have a literal, typological, *and* allegorical meaning at the same time. For example, the story of the Exodus refers to the literal deliverance of Israel from bondage in Egypt. It is also a type of the deliverance wrought by Christ on the Cross (another historical event). Finally, it may also be interpreted allegorically, as the deliverance of the soul from sin. This latter method is used frequently during Great Lent, when the hymnographers invite us to put ourselves in the place of Old Testament characters and see their struggles as an allegory of our own, personal spiritual journey.

CHAPTER FIVE

Reflection

1. Who is the father of the People of Israel?

2. What did God promise to him concerning his offspring?

3. In what way was the Passover Lamb slain at the time of the Exodus a foreshadowing of Christ?

4. To whom did God reveal the Ten Commandments and the instructions for proper worship?

5. What did Israel believe about God that set her apart from other nations?

6. What does the word *prophecy* literally mean?

7. How do the prophets foreshadow the work of Christ?

8. What was the job of the high priest in the Old Testament? How is this related to the work of Christ?

9. Which Old Testament figure is a type or figure of the kingship of Christ?

10. What is the method of biblical interpretation whereby the history of Israel is interpreted in the light of the coming of Israel's Messiah?

Chapter Six

The Incarnation

Jesus Christ is the eternal Son and Word of God Who, without suffering any change to His divinity, became man and restored humanity to its original glory.

Once, while walking with His Disciples, Jesus asked them, *"Whom do men say that I the Son of Man am?"* (Matthew 16:13 ff.). They answered, *"Some say that Thou art John the Baptist: some, Elias; and others, Jeremias, or one of the prophets."* The world has never been at a loss for opinions concerning Christ. He has been called everything from a great moral philosopher and religious genius to a fraud and deceiver to "the greatest salesman in the world." All of these views, to one degree or another, reflect the hopes and fears of those who hold them, for we human beings have the unfortunate tendency to see in Christ whatever it is we want to see. But what about the real Jesus? What is the truth about this itinerant preacher from Galilee?

After hearing all of these different theories about His identity, Jesus then asked his Disciples, *"But Whom say ye that I am?"* In one way or another, this question is asked of every human being. It is the most important question that we will ever be asked, for the answer will determine our eternal destiny. What we believe about Jesus Christ determines how we will relate—or fail to relate—to Him. If Jesus was just a man like any of us, no more or no less, then what we think of Him matters very little. If, however, Jesus is Who He claimed to be, our relationship to Him is of decisive importance.

To this all-important question, Simon answered, *"Thou art the Christ, the Son of the living God."* By confessing Jesus to be the "Christ," Simon acknowledged Him to be the long-expected Messiah of Israel, the hope of all the world. By confessing Him to be the "Son of the Living God," he acknowledged Jesus to be God. Since we have already examined Christ's role as Messiah, let us focus on the second aspect of Simon's Confession: the divinity of Jesus Christ.

The fact that Jesus Christ is the Son of God means that He is One of the Holy Trinity—the eternal Son of the Father. Christ is not merely a messenger from God, but God Himself, Who became man for our salvation. At His conception by the Most Blessed Virgin Mary, the eternal Son and Word of God took upon Himself our human nature in its entirety and became man: *And the Word was made flesh, and dwelt among us* (John 1:14). Thus, Jesus Christ is both God and man. The Church's teaching about this is called the doctrine of the Incarnation (meaning "enfleshment") and may be summarized in this way:

> 1) Jesus Christ is One of the Holy Trinity, the eternal Son and Word of God the Father. When He became man, He did not cease being God. We have already seen that each person of the Trinity is

THE INCARNATION

"catholic"; that is, each sums up within Himself the whole of the Godhead. Thus, when we encounter Christ, we encounter God Himself: *For in Him dwelleth all the fullness of the Godhead bodily* (Colossians 2:9).

2) Christ became a real man, having a human body and rational soul. There is no essential aspect of human nature in which Christ did not share: *Wherefore in all things it behoved Him to be made like unto His brethren, that He might be a merciful and faithful High Priest in things pertaining to God, to make reconciliation for the sins of the people* (Hebrews 2:17).

3) In becoming man, Christ assumed human nature in its entirety. Because man is created in the image of the Holy Trinity, each human being sums up within himself the totality of human nature. Thus, Christ as man is united essentially to every man. He is one with the Father and the Holy Spirit according to His divinity, and one with each of us according to His humanity.

4) The divine and human natures in Christ remain distinct. When God became man, His divinity did not swallow up His humanity, but rather perfected it and made it what it was originally intended to be. According to the decree of the Council of Chalcedon (A.D. 451), the divine and human natures in Christ exist "without mixture or confusion." That which is divine remains divine, and that which is human remains human; but the human now exists in a divine way, because it is united with the divine.

5) Jesus Christ is one person, not two. Although the two natures of Christ remain distinct, they are united "without separation or division" (Chalcedon). This is so because the principle of their union is the one person of the Son. In His person, the Son and Word of God took upon Himself our human nature and made it His own. The Word did not "adopt" or attach Himself to an already existing man named Jesus. On the contrary, the Word *is* the man Jesus! *What* is Jesus? He is both God and man. *Who* is Jesus? He is the eternal Son of God, One of the Holy Trinity.

When Simon correctly answered the question, "Who am I?," Jesus looked at him and said,

> *"Blessed art thou, Simon Barjona: for flesh and blood hath not revealed it unto thee, but My Father Who is in heaven. And I say also unto thee, that thou art Peter, and upon this rock I will build My Church, and the gates of hades shall not prevail against it."*

There are two aspects of Jesus' response to Simon Peter's confession that merit attention. First of all, Jesus states that Peter did not come to this knowledge by himself or by means of human investigation. Indeed, it is impossible to penetrate into the mystery of Christ solely by the light of unaided human reason. The true nature of Christ's person is inaccessible to the inquiries of historical research. That is why all attempts to find the "historical Jesus" apart from the Christ presented in the Gospels have ended in utter failure.

True knowledge of Christ comes only by revelation of God. Thus, the Church's teaching about the nature of

THE INCARNATION

Christ is not based upon the opinion of men, but upon God's self-revelation to mankind in the person of His Son. Christ reveals the Father to man (cf. Matthew 11:27), and the Father confirms that Christ is indeed His Son. At both the Baptism and the Transfiguration of Christ, a voice from heaven proclaimed, *"This is My beloved Son"* (Mat 3:17; 17:5). Thus, God the Father Himself witnesses to the divinity of Christ.

In addition to the witness of the Father, the Holy Spirit also bears witness to Christ (cf. John 15:26). St. Paul states that no man can genuinely call Jesus "Lord" except by the power of the Holy Spirit (1 Corinthians 12:3). Thus, our knowledge of Christ is not dependent upon our limited faculties or the paucity of historical data, but upon the witness of God:

> *If we receive the witness of men, the witness of God is greater: for this is the witness of God which He hath testified of His Son. He that believeth on the Son of God hath the witness in himself: He that believeth not God hath made him a liar; because he believeth not the record that God gave of His Son. And this is the record, that God hath given to us eternal life, and this life is in His Son* (1 John 5:9-11).

The second important aspect of Jesus' reply is the connection He drew between Peter's confession and the establishment of the Church. Jesus renamed Simon "Peter" (*Petros*, a rock) and stated, *"upon this rock (Petra, a large rock) I will build My Church."*

Even before the Protestant Reformation, there was a disagreement between those who said the Church is built upon Peter himself and those who said She is built upon the *fact* that Jesus is the Christ (that is, Peter's confession). This battle of interpretations, however, is a false problem, for genuine faith cannot be separated from the one who holds it. The fact is that Peter is the one who confessed Jesus to be the Son of God, and it was to Peter (and later to the other Apostles) that Christ gave the keys to the kingdom (Matthew 16:19). Faith in Christ is not an abstract philosophical proposition but a relationship with Him, and this relationship is the life of the Church.

It is not enough for us to believe that Jesus is the Son of God, One of the Holy Trinity made flesh. In the Creed, we do not say that we believe *that* there is one God. Rather, we say, "I believe *in* one God . . . " Between belief *that* and belief *in* there is a world of difference — the difference between heaven and hell. The Apostle James wrote, *Thou believest that there is one God; thou doest well: the devils also believe, and tremble* (James 2:19). A truly Orthodox confession of the doctrine of Christ must come from the innermost heart; it must come out of a living relationship with Him.

For this reason it is pointless to try to separate Peter from his confession. In spite of his falls, Peter's confession became his life — even to the point of dying a martyr's death for the One Whom he confessed to be the Son of God.

If we are to be true Orthodox Christians, our confession must be like that of Peter. We must pass beyond knowledge *about* Christ to an intimate, personal knowledge *of* Christ. To be sure, Peter was not perfect, and in this we may take some consolation in the midst of our

THE INCARNATION

imperfections. There were times when he doubted and even denied Christ, and yet he always came back to the One Whom he had confessed, the One Whom he knew to be the Son of God.

THE FATHERS SPEAK

You know what happens when a portrait that has been painted on a panel becomes obliterated through external stains. The artist does not throw away the panel, but the subject of the portrait has to come and sit for it again, and then the likeness is re-drawn on the same material. Even so was it with the All-holy Son of God. He, the Image of the Father, came and dwelt in our midst, in order that He might renew mankind after Himself, and seek out His lost sheep, even as He says in the Gospel: I came to seek and to save that which was lost. This also explains His saying to the Jews: "Except a man be born anew." . . . He was not referring to a man's natural birth from his mother, as they thought, but to the re-birth and re-creation of the soul in the image of God.

St. Athanasius the Great
from *On the Incarnation*

Therefore we acknowledge our Lord Jesus Christ, the Only-begotten Son of God, perfect God and perfect man, consisting of rational soul and body: in respect to His divinity, begotten of the Father before the ages; in

CHAPTER SIX

respect to His humanity, begotten also of the Virgin Mary, for us and for our salvation. He is also of one substance (nature) with the Father in respect to His divinity, and of one substance with us in respect to His humanity, for a unity of two natures has come about. Therefore, we acknowledge one Christ, one Son, one Lord. In accordance with this principle of the union without confusion, we acknowledge the Holy Virgin as Mother of God (Theotokos), because the Word was incarnate and made man, and from the very conception united to Himself the temple taken from her.

St. Cyril of Alexandria
from *Epistle 39*
The Later Christian Fathers

He Who is comes to be; the uncreated is created, the unconfinable is confined, through the mediation of the intellectual soul, the bridge between the divinity and the grossness of the flesh. He Who enriches becomes poor: He takes upon Himself the poverty of my flesh so that I may receive the riches of His divinity. He who is full is emptied: He is emptied of His own glory for a little while, that I may share in His fullness. . . . What a mystery is this, concerned with me! I had my share in the divine image, and I did not preserve it. He shares in my flesh in order that He may rescue the image and confer immortality on the flesh.

St. Gregory the Theologian
from *Oration 38*
The Later Christian Fathers

THE INCARNATION
Special Study
Icon of the Invisible God

When God gave the Ten Commandments to Moses, He specifically outlawed the making of idols. He did so to prevent the People of Israel from creating an image of God from their imaginations. As the Apostle Paul said, *We ought not to think that the Godhead is like unto gold, or silver, or stone, graven by art and man's device* (Acts 17:29). God is pure spirit; He has no material form. When the writers of the Scriptures speak of the "hand" of God or state that God "sees" or "hears," they are using metaphorical language. While God allowed this kind of language about Him to be used—how else could we speak about God?—He drew the line at material representations. God understood that man had the tendency to formulate gods in his own fallen image. The prohibition against idols was a safeguard against thinking that man could somehow "capture" the infinite God by using created forms.

The Law of Moses, however, was a custodian or school master (cf. Galatians 3:24). Its purpose was to prepare the world for the coming of Christ. With the advent of the Son of God in the flesh, man's relationship with God changed radically, for *no man hath seen God at any time; the Only-begotten Son, Who is in the bosom of the Father, He hath declared Him* (John 1:18). Jesus

CHAPTER SIX

Christ, *the Icon of the invisible God* (Colossians 1:15), came to reveal God to man and to renew in man the image of God which had been distorted by sin. At the Incarnation, the bodiless God took on a body; the invisible One became visible to human eyes.

Iconography is the one of the ways the Church expresses Her faith in the Incarnation. Icons are not merely helpful "illustrations," they witness to the fact that the invisible God has become man. St. John of Damascus wrote:

> I do not adore the creation rather than the Creator, but I adore the One Who became a creature, Who was formed as I was, Who clothed Himself in creation without weakening or departing from His divinity, that He might raise our nature in glory and make us partakers of His divine nature. . . . Therefore I boldly draw an image of the invisible God, not as invisible, but as having become visible for our sakes by partaking of flesh and blood. I do not draw an image of the immortal Godhead, but I paint the image of God Who became visible in the flesh (*On the Divine Images*).

Icons are the visual equivalents of the Divine Scriptures. Just as the Bible is not simply a book, so icons are not simply pictures. They are vehicles of revelation, sacraments of God's presence. St. Theodore the Studite wrote:

> [Jesus] nowhere told anyone to write down the "concise word," yet His image was drawn in writing by the Apostles and has been preserved up to the present. Whatever is marked there with paper

THE INCARNATION

and ink, the same is marked on the icon with varied pigments or some other material medium.

Just as we encounter Christ in the Scriptures, so we also encounter Christ and His Saints in the holy icons.

The Seventh Ecumenical Council (A.D. 787) decreed that the Church must proclaim Her faith in the Incarnate Lord "in words and in images." In doing so, She safeguards Herself from those who would deny that Jesus Christ is God in the flesh. On the first Sunday of Great Lent—the "Sunday of Orthodoxy"—the Church commemorates the final restoration of icons after the period of iconoclasm (A.D. 843). On this day the Church reaffirms Her commitment to proclaim the whole counsel of God (cf. Acts 20:27) and to hold fast to the apostolic tradition *delivered once for all to the Saints* (Jude 3). Icons, therefore, are not a matter of "decoration" but are an essential element of the Orthodox Faith.

Because of the doctrinal importance of icons, the Church has developed strict rules, or canons, concerning their creation. Not every "religious" picture can be considered an icon. Above all, an icon must convey the inner spiritual meaning of the person or event depicted. The beauty of an icon stems not from the physical beauty of the subject but from the inner beauty of a life transformed by divine grace. The Son of God came to restore the divine image in man. Iconography is the graphic witness to this restoration.

CHAPTER SIX

Reflection

1. Who is Jesus Christ?

2. Was there ever a time when He did not exist?

3. Did the Word of God cease to be God when He became man?

4. Did the Word of God adopt an already existing man in which to dwell?

5. Did the Word of God inhabit a human body (without a soul) in the same way that a person dwells in a house?

6. If the Word of God became a particular man, how is He related to the rest of us?

7. Using the words *person* and *nature*, complete the following sentences:

   In the Holy Trinity, three co-equal [   ] exist in one, undivided [   ].

   In Christ, two complete and perfect [   ] exist in one and the same [   ].

8. Who was the first to confess that Jesus is "the Christ, the Son of the living God"?

9. What is the difference between belief *that* Christ is God and belief *in* Christ?

10. How does the Incarnation affect the Old Testament prohibition of images?

CHAPTER SEVEN

Mankind's "Yes" to God

The Virgin Mary, in her purity of heart and perfect receptivity to the will of God, is the historical foundation of our salvation and the fulfillment of the purpose of humanity.

Fr. Georges Florovsky wrote, "To ignore the Mother of God means to misinterpret the Son." Mariology—what the Church believes about the Most Blessed Virgin Mary—and Christology—what She believes about Christ—are inseparable. One without the other will inevitably lead to a distortion of the Christian Faith. Unfortunately, this is precisely what has happened in western Christendom, thanks to the Protestant Reformation.

At the Third Ecumenical Council (Ephesus, A.D. 431), the holy Fathers sanctioned the widespread practice of hymning the Blessed Virgin as *Theotokos*, which means "God-bearer" or "Mother of God." They did so to preserve the correct understanding of Christ as God made man. They realized that what was at stake was not some optional aspect of personal piety, but the very substance of the Christian Faith. What we believe about the Virgin Mary invariably affects what we believe

CHAPTER SEVEN

about Christ. Thus, a proper understanding of Mary is essential for mankind's salvation.

First of all, a correct Mariology underscores the fact that Christ is One of the Holy Trinity and not merely a man somehow joined to God. Although Christ was both fully God and fully man, He is one and only one person: the eternal Son and Word of God. A man, even one intimately united with God, could not save humanity and raise us up to the perfect participation in the life of God. Only God could renew His image in man and impart unto him the fullness of His divine life. If Christ is not God, then our salvation is an illusion. Therefore, to confess that the Blessed Virgin is the Mother of God is to confess that the Son born of her is God Himself, One of the Holy Trinity. On the other hand, to deny that Mary is the Theotokos is to deny that Christ is truly God and, therefore, to deny the possibility of our salvation.

Secondly, the proper understanding of the person and work of the Virgin Mary is necessary to safeguard the reality of Christ's human nature. Some suppose that the Blessed Virgin was merely a passive "channel" or "passageway" through which God entered the world. Such a notion, however, makes the humanity of Christ an illusion. The Church confesses that Mary was the mother of the incarnate God in every sense of the term. Christ took the substance of His humanity from her, becoming in her womb what He was not so that mankind might become what He is:

> In Him and through Him are we saved, and together with Gabriel let us cry aloud unto the Virgin:

MAN'S "YES" TO GOD

Rejoice, thou who art full of grace! The Lord is with thee! From thee has Christ our God and our Salvation taken human nature, raising it up unto Himself (*The Festal Menaion*).

In addition, the confession of Mary as the Theotokos affirms the "human dimension" of our salvation. Man was created in the image of God. This means that he was given the freedom either to realize his life as love and communion with God or to deny his divine vocation and condemn himself to an egoistic hell of his own making. Even though the image of God in man has been severely marred by the Fall, it has not been totally obliterated. Although man finds himself enslaved to sin and death, he nonetheless retains the capacity—however limited—to respond to God. Without this capacity it would be impossible for man to be saved, for salvation is a free, personal participation in the life of God. God will not, indeed cannot, save man against his will. Only God can save man, but man must want to be saved. He must respond to God and enter into the life which God offers him.

When the Church confesses the most holy Virgin to be the Mother of God, She is affirming the freedom which mankind possesses to respond to God and to accept the life that He offers. To hear some Protestant commentators talk about the Incarnation, one would get the idea that Mary had absolutely nothing to do with it. The logical implication of such an approach is that God simply "used" the Maiden as an inanimate tool.

CHAPTER SEVEN

The fact of the matter is that the Virgin had the freedom, in modern parlance, to "just say, 'No!'" She could have refused the joyous tidings of the Archangel; she could have rejected God's plan for the salvation of mankind. Yet she—alone among the sons and daughters of Eve—said, "Yes," to God with such purity of heart that she became a vessel fit to hold the uncontainable God. *Behold the Handmaid of the Lord, be it unto me according to thy word* (Luke 1:38). Mary's "Yes"—her *fiat*—is the foundation of our salvation. To better understand this, let us consider the historical, cosmic, and ethical dimensions of the Virgin's "Yes."

We have seen that the coming of Christ was the fruit of a long, historical process. God prepared the world for the coming of His Son by electing the children of Abraham as His own People. To Israel God gave the Law, the priesthood, and the prophets. Therefore, Christ—the fulfillment of the Law, the priesthood, and the prophets—cannot be separated from this historical process.

The most blessed Virgin Mary is the culmination of all that God has done through Israel to prepare the world for the coming of His Son. She is the perfect flower of God's plan of salvation, for from her immaculate womb "flowered forth the Fruit of Life"—Christ, our true God!

> He Who promised to thy forefather David that of the fruit of his body He would set upon the throne of his kingdom, He it is Who has chosen thee, the only excellency of Jacob, to be His spiritual dwelling place.

MAN'S "YES" TO GOD

God promised to our forefather Abraham that in his seed the Gentiles would be blessed, O pure Lady, and through thee today the promise receives its fulfillment.

The Holy Scriptures speak of thee mystically, O Mother of the Most High. For Jacob saw in days of old the ladder that prefigured thee, and said: "This is the stair on which God shall tread" (cf. Genesis 28:12-17). Therefore, as is right, dost thou hear the salutation: Rejoice, thou who art full of grace! The Lord is with thee (*The Festal Menaion*).

The Virgin Mary, however, not only stands at the end of a long historical process, she is also the culmination of the entire human race and of all creation. "All of creation rejoices in thee, O full of grace!" One hymn states, "He [Christ] was born of the Father before eternity without a mother, but now for our sake He came from thee [the Virgin] without a father!" Commenting on this hymn, Paul Evdokimov has written, "The analogy is clearly described: the maternity of the Virgin presents itself as the human figure of the paternity of God. If fatherhood is the category of divine life, motherhood is the religious category of human life" (*The Sacrament of Love*, pp. 34-35).

The Virgin Mary, therefore, is the perfect icon of how humanity—if it is to be truly human—ought to respond to God. To quote Evdokimov again: "The Bible exalts woman as the instrument of spiritual receptivity in human nature . . . its capacity to receive the divine" (p. 35).

CHAPTER SEVEN

It is not accidental that the Book of Genesis records that Eve, and not Adam, was the first to eat of the forbidden fruit. If man as the priest of creation has failed to offer the world to God in love, it is because of his failure to receive all that God has given him in love. This is the failure of the "feminine principle" of humanity, the failure of Eve. In the person of the Theotokos, however, humanity is renewed, for she is the New Eve—the perfect human response to God.

In the services for the Annunciation, many of the hymns are in the form of a dialogue between Mary and Gabriel. Mary is hesitant at first, fearful of being led astray: "I am afraid. I fear lest thou deceive me, as Eve was deceived, and lead me far from God." In the end, however, she is convinced by the truth of the Archangel's words and commits herself to God: *"Behold the Handmaid of the Lord, be it unto me according to thy word."* Mary's "Yes" is the answer to Eve's "No". Through her receptivity to God, Christ—our true High Priest—came into the world to offer all of creation back to God in one all-encompassing sacrifice of love.

In this way, Mary's "Yes" is the "Yes" of all humanity to God. One of the hymns for the Nativity expresses it this way:

> What shall we offer Thee, O Christ, Who for our sakes hast appeared on earth as man? Every creature made by Thee offers Thee thanks. The angels offer Thee a hymn; the heavens a star; the Magi, gifts; the shepherds, their wonder; the earth, its cave; the wilderness, the manger; and we offer Thee a Virgin Mother (*The Festal Menaion*)!

MAN'S "YES" TO GOD

If, therefore, the Virgin is the historical foundation of our salvation and indeed fulfills the most basic purpose of humanity as a whole, then she rightly serves as a model for our own lives. Our task as Orthodox Christians is to strive to respond to God in every way as did the Virgin Theotokos. Archimandrite George of Mt. Athos writes,

> Contemporary man is deluded by the devil and believes—as did Adam and Eve earlier—that his freedom is to be found in his autonomy and in his revolt against God. With this egoistic attitude man loses the possibility of true communion, not only with his God and Father, but also with his fellow men, and he lives as an orphan in an intolerable loneliness, which he experiences as an existential emptiness (*The Eros of Repentance,* pp. 70-71).

If we are to find our true freedom as persons created in the image of God, we must follow the example of our most blessed Lady and say "Yes" to God in every facet of our lives. "Calling to mind our most holy, most pure, most blessed and glorious Lady, the Theotokos and Ever-virgin Mary, with all the Saints, let us commend ourselves, one another, and all our life unto Christ our God!" In this way, we will begin to bear Christ within ourselves, as the Apostle Paul says, *My little children, of whom I travail in birth again until Christ be formed in you* (Galatians 4:19).

CHAPTER SEVEN
THE FATHERS SPEAK

Eve, by her disobedience, brought death upon herself and on all the human race. Mary, by her obedience, brought salvation.

Eve had to be recapitulated in Mary so that a virgin might be the intercessor for a virgin, and by the obedience of a virgin, undo and overcome the disobedience of a virgin.

St. Irenaios of Lyons
from *The Preaching of the Apostles*

In her virginity Eve put on leaves of shame. Your Mother put on, in her virginity, the garment of glory that suffices for all. I gave the small mantle of the body to the One Who covers all.

Blessed are you also, Mary, whose name is great and exalted because of your Child. Indeed, you were able to say how much and how and where the Great One, Who became small, dwelt in you.

St. Ephrem the Syrian
from *Hymns on the Nativity*

Thou hast contained in thy womb, O Virgin Mother, One of the Trinity, Christ the King, Whose praises all creation sings and before Whom the thrones on high tremble. O All-venerated Lady, entreat Him for the salvation of our souls.

St. Andrew of Crete
from the *Canon on the Nativity of the Theotokos*
The Festal Menaion
Faber and Faber, 1969

MAN'S "YES" TO GOD
Special Study
Fervent Intercessors

While our Lord was hanging from the Cross, pouring out His life for the salvation of the world, He looked down upon His most pure Mother and the Apostle John and said to the holy Virgin, *"Woman, behold thy son."* To John He said, *"Behold thy mother"* (John 19:26-27). From this time forth, the Virgin maiden who had given birth to God in the flesh was to be the mother of His Disciples. Just as Eve was the "Mother of all the living," so the Virgin is the "Mother of all Christians," the personification of Holy Mother Church. To those who are united to her Son through Holy Baptism, she extends her motherly embrace.

As our Mother, the All-holy Theotokos intercedes for us before the Throne of Her Son. As our fervent Intercessor and constant Advocate before the Creator, the Virgin never tires and never fails to remember her spiritual children in her prayers. When we are at our lowest ebb and feel as though we have been forsaken by all the world, we may take courage in the fact that our Lady is ever ready to come to us and intercede for us, winning greater strength for all who call upon her Son in faith.

Since the time of the Protestant Reformation, however, much of Western Christendom has either ignored or rejected outright the intercession of the Mother of God and the Saints for those on earth. In doing so, Protestants have forfeited one of the greatest privileges of

CHAPTER SEVEN

being Christians. The Apostle James enjoins us to pray for one another, and in the same verse, explains why: *the effectual fervent prayer of a righteous man availeth much* (James 5:16). It is ironic that those who oppose the idea of seeking the intercession of the Saints in heaven have no objections to asking ordinary, sinful Christians to pray for them. But let us consider whose prayers, according to St. James, are more effectual: those Christians still alive on earth struggling with their own sins and problems, or those who have gone on to be with God and are recognized by the Church for their holiness of life?

The Saints are those who have passed through this life in victorious faith and now behold the face of Christ. United with Him in love, they exist in a state of perfect accord with His holy will. Thus, we may be assured that when they pray for us who are on earth, their supplications are in complete harmony with the purposes of God. No longer capable of being deceived by the wiles of the devil, they form a mighty army, joining their will to the will of God and standing firm with us as we fight the good fight of faith. If God hears the prayers of ordinary Christians embroiled in the trials of life (and He certainly does), then how much more does He heed the intercessions of those who have pleased Him most, whom He has called to be with Himself in heaven.

I am the God of Abraham, and the God of Isaac, and the God of Jacob. God is not the God of the dead, but of the living (Matthew 22:32). In Christ, death is no longer the impenetrable barrier which separates us from those who have gone on before us. Indeed, the writer of Hebrews affirms that the Saints in heaven are aware of what is going on in our lives:

> *Wherefore seeing we also are compassed about with so great a cloud of witnesses, let us lay aside every weight, and the sin which doth so easily beset us, and let us run with patience the race that is set before us* (Hebrews 12:1).

The Saints not only cheer us on as we run the race of life, they actively participate in our race as they intercede for us, winning greater strength for all who battle evil. Our All-holy Lady, the Theotokos, stands at the head of this chorus of Saints and remains for us on earth our steadfast Protectress and constant Advocate before the Creator:

> **Steadfast Protectress of Christians, constant Advocate before the Creator, despise not the cry of us sinners, but in thy goodness come speedily to help us who call on thee in faith. Hasten to hear our petition and to intercede for us, O Theotokos, for thou dost always protect those who honor thee.**

CHAPTER SEVEN

Reflection

1. What does the name *Theotokos* mean?

2. How did the Archangel greet the Virgin at the Annunciation?

3. In what way is the Virgin the culmination of the history of Israel?

4. In what way is the Virgin as a woman representative of the whole human race?

5. In what way is the Virgin mankind's offering to God?

6. What is the relationship of the Virgin to Eve?

7. What did the Virgin say to the Archangel Gabriel in response to his message?

8. How does the Virgin's response serve as a model for our own lives?

9. What is the relationship between the Virgin and the Church on earth?

10. Does the Virgin take an active part in our lives?

Chapter Eight
The Teachings of Christ

To live the life that Christ came to give us, we must be willing to follow His commandments, which is the way of suffering love.

Throughout His ministry, Jesus was called *Rabbi*, which means teacher. Although Jesus gained fame as a miracle worker, He was especially known for His teachings. Indeed, today virtually all of the world's religions recognize Jesus Christ as a great religious teacher. Even atheists admire His ethical teachings. Yet most of the people who find Jesus to be such an "enlightened" teacher have never actually bothered to study His teachings. They merely summarize them in terms of the "golden rule" or "love thy neighbor" — sayings which they then reinterpret in light of their own beliefs.

This attitude creates the nonthreatening, low-calorie, "gentle Jesus, meek and mild" that has become so popular in our day. In His own day, however, Jesus' teachings were not always well received. The religious establishment perceived them precisely as a threat to its beliefs and way of life.

Jesus' teachings were controversial not only because He, Himself, claimed to be God, but also because

CHAPTER EIGHT

He told men that there was only one thing in life worth having—the kingdom of God—and that it would cost a man all that had in order to acquire it. *Again, the kingdom of heaven is like unto a merchant man, seeking goodly pearls: Who, when he had found one pearl of great price, went and sold all that he had, and bought it* (Matthew 13:45-46). The people of Jesus' time, not unlike people of our own day, did not want to hear this. They were not interested in giving up their lives in order to acquire that life which has no end. They simply wanted a set of rules to follow that would guarantee them a happy, peaceful life.

The ethical teachings of the Orthodox Church, faithfully based upon the teachings of Her Lord, are concerned with one thing only: to lead man to the kingdom of heaven. She knows that there is only one path to heaven: to keep the commandments of Christ. And yet, the commandments of Christ are not just another set of rules to follow—a Christian replacement for the Old Testament Law. On the contrary, they are a new way of life, a new way of experiencing one's relationship with God, with others, and with the whole creation. They have as their aim neither the ethical improvement of man's behavior nor the moral justification of his actions, but the transformation of man's life into the likeness of God.

In the Sermon on the Mount, Jesus gave His Disciples the commandment which most clearly expresses the purpose for man's existence and the purpose for Christ's work on earth: *Be ye therefore perfect, even as your Father Who is in heaven is perfect* (Matthew 5:48). Thus, we are commanded to attain unto the state of perfect Godlikeness; anything less than this is sin and failure, that is, *missing the mark.*

As the Fall enslaved mankind to a way of life contrary to its true nature, so the coming of Christ once again opened the gates of paradise and made it possible for man to live as he was originally intended to live. To follow Christ, therefore, is to live (or at least try to live) the new life which He came to give to mankind. It is not a matter of earning "merits" or trying to "make up" for past sins, but of entering into a new way of living in the image of God. *If thou wilt enter into life, keep the commandments* (Matthew 19:17).

There are two aspects of Jesus' teachings that we must understand if we are to faithfully keep His commandments. First, following the commandments of Christ means that one must go beyond the letter of the Law. Jesus insisted that He had not come to destroy the Law of Moses, but to fulfill it (Matthew 5:17). In fulfilling the Law, Jesus penetrated into the inner spirit of the Law, and He expects us to do the same. *For I say unto you, That except your righteousness shall exceed the righteousness of the scribes and Pharisees, ye shall in no case enter into the kingdom of heaven* (Matthew 5:20). It is not enough for us to merely follow some external rules.

Jesus gave several examples of going beyond the letter of the Law:

> *Ye have heard that it was said by them of old time, Thou shalt not kill; and whosoever shall kill shall be in danger of the judgment: But I say unto you, That whosoever is angry with his brother without a cause shall be in danger*

CHAPTER EIGHT

of the judgment: and whosoever shall say to his brother, "Raca," shall be in danger of the council: but whosoever shall say, "Thou fool," shall be in danger of hell fire. Therefore if thou bring thy gift to the altar, and there rememberest that thy brother hath ought against thee; Leave there thy gift before the altar, and go thy way; first be reconciled to thy brother, and then come and offer thy gift (Matthew 5:21-24).

Here, Jesus internalizes the commandment against murder and shows us that hatred, bitterness, and unjust anger are also grave sins. We cannot justify ourselves before God by saying, "Well, I never killed anyone."

Jesus goes on to do the same with the commandment against adultery. He teaches us that it is not only the physical act of adultery which is a sin, but the desire itself:

Ye have heard that it was said by them of old time, "Thou shalt not commit adultery." But I say unto you, that whosoever looketh on a woman to lust after her hath committed adultery with her already in his heart (Matthew 5:27-28).

God sees into the depth of our being and knows the sinful attitudes and dispositions that dwell there. If we are to follow Christ, we must deal first and foremost with these attitudes and dispositions.

In addition, to follow the commandments of Christ is to walk the narrow path of self-denial. There is no way that we can live the life that Christ came to give us if we are living in a self-centered way. Our Lord made it very clear that those who wish to follow Him must sacrifice everything in order to enter into His blessings:

THE TEACHINGS OF CHRIST

If any man will come after Me, let him deny himself, and take up his Cross daily, and follow Me. For whosoever will save his life shall lose it: but whosoever will lose his life for My sake, the same shall save it. For what is a man advantaged, if he gain the whole world, and lose himself, or be cast away? For whosoever shall be ashamed of Me and of My words, of him shall the Son of Man be ashamed, when He shall come in His own glory, and in His Father's, and of the holy angels (Luke 9:23-26).

Jesus commanded that any obstacle which stands between us and the kingdom of heaven must be removed:

And if thy right eye offend thee, pluck it out, and cast it from thee: for it is profitable for thee that one of thy members should perish, and not that thy whole body should be cast into hell. And if thy right hand offend thee, cut it off, and cast it from thee: for it is profitable for thee that one of thy members should perish, and not that thy whole body should be cast into hell (Matthew 5:29-30).

This does not mean that we should physically maim ourselves, but rather that we must be willing to give up anything which leads to sin, even those things which may be perfectly good in and of themselves. In other words, we have to make some sacrifices for the sake of our spiritual well-being. There are no shortcuts to holiness.

All of this is done ultimately for the sake of love. We must deny ourselves for the sake of the love of God and of our fellow man. Needless to say, this kind of love is not an emotion or a feeling, but the dynamic gift of our life to another. Jesus said, *Greater love hath no man*

CHAPTER EIGHT

than this, that a man lay down his life for his friends (John 15:13). This is the very love that God has shown toward us:

> *Herein is love, not that we loved God, but that He loved us, and sent His Son to be the propitiation for our sins. Beloved, if God so loved us, we ought also to love one another. No man hath seen God at any time. If we love one another, God dwelleth in us, and His love is perfected in us* (1 John 4:10-12).

It is very popular in our day to talk about "love." However, the world's idea of love is that of self-satisfaction, not self-sacrifice. Often, "I love you" means "I love me and want you." This is not love, but the devil's parody of love. Those who preach an ethical system based on a love that knows no self-denial or sacrifice are preaching the doctrine of Antichrist. Do not be misled by these wolves in sheep's clothing. Love that does not demand the total gift of oneself is not love at all. St. James makes this point especially clear:

> *If a brother or sister be naked, and destitute of daily food, and one of you say unto them, "Depart in peace, be ye warmed and filled;" notwithstanding ye give them not those things which are needful to the body; what doth it profit* (James 2:15-16)?

Thus, the way of Christ is the way of the Cross. There is no other way to the resurrection and to eternal life but through the sacrifice of suffering love. Of course, our own suffering and self-sacrifice would be pointless were it not for suffering of Christ. It is His life that gives meaning to our life. It is His sacrifice on the Cross which makes our life of self-denial worthwhile.

THE TEACHINGS OF CHRIST

No amount of human suffering could possibly heal the great wounds caused by sin; only the suffering and death of God Himself could do that. Ultimately, we are able to follow the commandments of Christ only because He has first lived human life the way it was meant to be lived.

THE FATHERS SPEAK

It is in our power to persevere in that love, for it is not enough to love and experience its passion, but it is necessary as well to persevere in it and to add fuel to the fire so that it may persist, for this is to abide in love. All blessedness consists in this. To abide in love is to abide in God, and for him who abides in Him to possess Him, for it says, *he who abideth in love abideth in God, and God abideth in him* (1 John 4:16). This happens when we have love firmly fixed in the will, and arrive at that through the commandments and keep the laws of Him Whom we love. It is by actions that the soul is disposed towards one habit or the other, so that men may partake of goodness or wickedness, just as in the case of crafts we acquire skills and learn them by becoming accustomed to their exercise. God's laws which apply to human activities and determine and order them towards Him alone impart the appropriate habit to those who act rightly, which is to will that which pleases the Lawgiver and to subject all our will to Him alone and to will nothing apart from Him. This alone is to know how to love properly, and for this reason the Savior says, *if you keep My commandments, you will abide in My love* (John 15:10).

CHAPTER EIGHT

If, then, to imitate Christ and to live according to Him is to live in Christ, this life is the effect of the will when it obeys God's purposes. Just as Christ subjected His human will to His divine will in order that He might leave us an example of the right life, so He did not refuse death on behalf of the world when it was necessary to die. But before the time came He prayed that it might not happen, showing that He did not please Himself by the things which He suffered, but as Paul says, *He became obedient* (Phil. 2:8) and went to the Cross, not as though He had one will, or one compounded out of two, but rather the agreement of two wills.

St. Nicholas Cabasilas
from *The Life in Christ*

The fear of hell trains beginners to flee from evil; the desire for the reward of good things gives to the advanced the eagerness for the practice of virtues. But the mystery of love removes the mind from all created things, causing it to be blind to all that is less than God. Only those who have become blind to all that is less than God does the Lord instruct by showing them more divine things.

St. Maximus the Confessor
from *The Four Centuries on Love*
Tr. by George Berthold
Paulist Press, 1985

THE TEACHINGS OF CHRIST
Special Study
Saving Humility

The goal of the Christian life is to become like God, Who is the very essence of love. To do so we must learn to love as He loves. Our whole outlook on life must change, and our will must be trained. Before we can attain the heights of divine love, we must first attain the spirit of genuine humility, which St. John Climacus calls the "door to the kingdom":

> Anyone who has acquired knowledge of self has come to understand the fear of the Lord, and walking with the help of this fear, he has arrived at the doorway of love. For humility is the door to the kingdom, opening up to those who come near (*The Ladder of Divine Ascent*).

One of the Desert Fathers defined humility as seeing oneself as being lower than all of creation. This is a radical concept for our modern society, which has raised the idea of "self-esteem" to almost cultic status. Nevertheless, the attainment such humility of spirit is essential for our salvation. *Learn of Me,* says our Lord Jesus Christ, *for I am meek and lowly in heart* (Matthew 11:29).

Humility is attained first of all through obedience. Obedience to God through obedience to the canons of the Church and to our spiritual father or mother cuts off our self-will. As in all things, our Lord is our exemplar, for He submitted himself completely to the will of His

CHAPTER EIGHT

Father: *For I came down from heaven, not to do Mine own will, but the will of Him that sent Me* (John 6:38); and again, *not as I will, but as Thou wilt* (Matthew 26:39).

The second method for attaining humility is the remembrance of one's own sinfulness. This is not the same as obsessing over one's sins and harboring a guilt complex. Sins that have been confessed and repented of are forgiven by God. Nevertheless, we must always be mindful of our sinfulness so that we do not become proud and begin to judge others. Our Lord warns us:

> *Judge not, that ye be not judged. For with what judgment ye judge, ye shall be judged. . . . And why beholdest thou the speck in thy brother's eye, but considerest not the beam that is in thine own eye* (Matthew 7:1-3)?

One of the most beautiful examples of such humility is that of St. Moses the Ethiopian. Moses was the leader of a band of robbers and was possibly even a murderer. He repented of his sins, however, and became a monk in the Egyptian desert of Scetis. Because he was well respected for his holiness, the fathers of the monastery sent for him one day to help judge a brother who had fallen into a sin. Abba Moses refused to go. Compelled by the fathers to attend the meeting, he took up a jug with a hole in it, filled it with water, and went to the meeting. When the fathers saw him carrying a leaking jug, they asked what he was doing. He replied, "My sins run out behind me, and I do not see them, and today I am coming to judge the errors of another." At this the fathers forgave the brother who had sinned and learned a lesson in Christlike humility (cf. *The Sayings of the Desert Fathers,* pp. 138ff.).

THE TEACHINGS OF CHRIST

Yet another way to attain humility is to read the lives of the Saints. When we read how the Martyrs suffered torture and death for the sake of Christ and how all of the Saints endured great hardships solely in order to attain the kingdom of heaven, we realize how very little we have actually done for the Lord. St. Hesychios wrote:

> True humility is also brought about by meditating daily on the achievements of our brethren, by extolling their natural superiorities and by comparing our gifts with theirs. When the intellect sees in this way how worthless we are and how far we fall short of the perfection of our brethren, we will regard ourselves as dust and ashes, and not as men but as some kind of cur, more defective in every respect and lower than all men on earth (*The Philokalia*, vol. 1).

When man attains true humility, he no longer experiences the commandments of Christ as an external law that constrains his will, but rather as a fount of genuine spiritual freedom welling up within him:

> Holy humility has this to say: "The one who loves me will not condemn someone, or pass judgment on anyone, or lord it over someone else, or show off his wisdom until he has been united with me. A man truly joined to me is no longer in bondage to the Law" (*The Ladder of Divine Ascent*).

CHAPTER EIGHT

Reflection

1. What is the one thing for which the wise man strives?

2. What is the goal of following the commandments of Christ?

3. Does man earn his salvation by following the commandments of Christ?

4. What is the relationship between the Law of Moses and the commandments of Christ?

5. Is it enough for us to strictly observe the letter of the Law?

6. Whom does Jesus say will save his own life?

7. Is there any sacrifice for the sake of the kingdom of heaven which is too great?

8. What is the relationship of love to self-denial?

9. What virtue is necessary in order to attain Godlike love?

10. What three methods help us to attain humility?

Chapter Nine
Love Stronger than Death

Through His Death, Resurrection, and Ascension, Christ, Who is the love of God incarnate, has destroyed the power of sin and death and has raised humanity to the right hand of God.

The essence of sin is the failure to love. In their rebellion, Adam and Eve refused the "divine love made food" offered to them by God, preferring instead life on their own. Cut off from loving communion with God, mankind has become enslaved to its own self-centeredness, the inevitable consequence of which is death. God, however, was not willing that the creature which bore His image should simply return back to the nothingness from which he was created:

> For Thou dost not wish, O Master, that the work of Thy hands should perish, neither dost Thou take pleasure in the destruction of men; but Thou desirest that all men should be saved and come to the knowledge of the truth (Prayer of St. Basil).

Yet only one thing could accomplish this: a love stronger than man's failure to love, ultimately, a love stronger than death (cf. Song of Songs 8:6).

If the fruit of Paradise was "divine love made food" for man, then Jesus Christ, the incarnate Son and Word of God, is "divine love made flesh." *For God so loved the world, that He gave His Only-begotten Son, that whosoever believeth in Him should not perish, but have everlasting life* (John 3:16). We have said that true love means the total gift of oneself to another, the emptying of oneself. Thus did God love us when the Son, being in the form of God, thought it not robbery to be equal with God: *But made Himself of no reputation, and took upon Him the form of a servant, and was made in the likeness of men: And being found in fashion as a man, He humbled Himself, and became obedient unto death, even the death of the Cross* (Philippians 2:6-8).

In our fallen existence, this profound self-emptying must inevitably take the form of sacrifice and suffering, for such love is no longer natural to us. This is why the Apostle Paul insists that the self-emptying of Christ was unto death, *even the death of the Cross*. It was not enough that God simply appear on earth as man and teach us a better way to live. For man to be healed of his sin and achieve the purpose for which he was created, this "divine Love made flesh" had to enter into the lowest depths of human existence. He had to partake, in His own person, of the ultimate consequences of man's sinfulness.

Man's rebellion could be healed only by divine obedience. Man's self-centeredness could be destroyed only by the divine self-sacrifice on the Cross. Man's enslavement to death and corruption could be loosed only by the Resurrection of Him Who has life in Himself (John 5:26). Finally, the limitations of man's created nature could be transcended only by ascending to heaven with Him Who first descended to earth (cf. Ephesians 4:9-10).

In the Garden of Gethsemane, shortly before His arrest, Jesus prayed that the cup of suffering might pass from Him. *Nevertheless*, He said, *not as I will, but as Thou wilt* (Matthew 26:39). When Christ took upon Himself our humanity from the Virgin, He assumed all natural aspects of human nature, including the human will. In His earthly life, the human will was inextricably joined with the divine will in perfect harmony.

This harmony reached its crescendo in the Garden of Gethsemane. St. Maximus the Confessor wrote:

> According to that which has come to pass for us, He became man as we are. He said humanly to His God and Father, "Not My will, but Thine which triumphs," for He Who was God by nature, had also, in as much as He was man, to will the accomplishment of the will of the Father (*Opsculum* 6).

Thus, in the Garden of Gethsemane, Christ overcame the disobedience of Adam through His human obedience to the will of God the Father.

After Jesus' arrest and trial at the hands of the Jewish leaders and the Roman governor, Pontius Pilate, He was beaten and mocked by the Roman soldiers. They robed Him in purple, the color of royalty, and placed upon His most pure head a crown of thorns. In this, Christ manifested the supreme humility of God and thereby conquered the pride of fallen man:

> He Who is King of the angels is arrayed in a crown of thorns. He Who wraps the heavens in clouds is

CHAPTER NINE

wrapped in the purple of mockery. He Who in Jordan set Adam free receives blows upon His face (*The Lenten Triodion*).

Upon the Cross, the love of God for mankind reached its apex as Christ descended to the lowest point of human existence: suffering and death. Here we see most clearly the great paradox of spiritual reality: God's glory is most abundantly manifest in His acceptance of human suffering. This self-emptying of God, for the sake of man, is the exact inverse of man's attempt to assume for himself the glory of God. By pouring out His most pure Blood upon the Cross, Christ not only blotted out the record of man's sin, but overcame the power by which sin holds mankind captive. Thus does the Cross of Christ destroy the power of man's rebellion.

It is important to note that the suffering and death of Christ was effective for man's salvation not merely because Christ was an "innocent" man unjustly slain, but because He was God. St. Gregory the Theologian wrote, "We needed an incarnate God, a God put to death, that we might live." Only God could take upon Himself the consequences of man's sin and thereby destroy them. Only God could enter the realm of death and fill it with His immortal life:

> He gave Himself as a ransom to death, in which we were held captive, sold under sin. Descending through the Cross into hades—that He might fill all things with Himself—He loosed the pangs of death. He arose on the third day, having made for all flesh a path to the resurrection from the dead, since it

was not possible for the Author of Life to be a victim of corruption (Liturgy of St. Basil).

The Resurrection of Christ frees all mankind from the bonds of corruption and death, because death had no power over Him Who is life and love Himself.

Forty days after His Resurrection, Christ gathered His Disciples at the Mt. of Olives (cf. Acts 1:1-11). Before their eyes He ascended into the heavens. With this, the economy of salvation came full circle: He "Who for us men and for our salvation came down from heaven," having lived a human life and died a human death, and having risen again victorious over death, now ascended back to His Father as both God and man: *no man hath ascended up to heaven, but He Who came down from heaven, even the Son of Man Who is in heaven* (John 3:13).

By assuming the entirety of our nature, Christ lived a perfect human life. In becoming man, Christ recreated the original image of God in man, which had become distorted through sin. *For we have not a High Priest Who cannot be touched with the feeling of our infirmities; but was in all points tempted like as we are, yet without sin* (Hebrews 4:15).

In dying a human death upon the Cross, He assumed the totality of man's rebellion. There was no consequence of man's Fall that Christ did not take upon Himself: *for He hath made Him to be sin for us, Who knew no sin; that we might be made the righteousness of God in Him* (2 Corinthians 5:21).

In rising from the dead, Christ brought with Himself the human nature that He had assumed and made it forever incorruptible. Because of the consubstantiality

CHAPTER NINE

of human nature, all men have a part in the resurrection of the dead:

> *But now is Christ risen from the dead, and become the firstfruits of them that slept. For since by man came death, by man came also the resurrection of the dead. For as in Adam all die, even so in Christ shall all be made alive* (1 Corinthians 15:20-22).

By ascending into heaven, Christ has taken our humanity and placed it forever at the right hand of God the Father. Man was originally created to become like God and reign eternally with Him. In Christ, human nature attains the purpose for which it was created:

> *Even when we were dead in sins, [God] hath quickened us together with Christ, (by grace ye are saved;) and hath raised us up together, and made us sit together in heavenly places in Christ Jesus* (Ephesians 2:5-6).

Just before His Ascension, Christ told His Disciples to wait in Jerusalem for the coming of the Holy Spirit. The Spirit is the promised Comforter (cf. John 14:6), Who guarantees Christ's abiding presence with His Disciples. The coming of the Spirit on Pentecost marked the birth of the Church, the Body of Christ. Thus, Jesus' last words on earth were about the founding of His Church.

As Jesus ascended, two angels appeared to the Disciples and told them that one day Christ would return in the same manner. The promise of the coming of the Spirit and the birth of the Church is therefore followed by the promise of Christ's return and the consummation of all things. Indeed, the Church lives precisely in this time between the Ascension of Christ and His Second Coming. Thus, the Church is both the remembrance of that which Christ has accomplished for us and the anticipation of His return in glory. But more than that, the Church is the living experience in the Holy Spirit of the saving work of Christ and of the glory which He has prepared for us. The remaining chapters of this book deal with this theme.

THE FATHERS SPEAK

Yesterday I was crucified with Him; today I am glorified with Him. Yesterday I died with Him; today I am made alive with Him. Yesterday I was buried with Him; today I am raised up with Him. Let us offer to Him Who suffered and rose again for us . . . ourselves, the possession most precious to God and most proper. Let us become like Christ, since He became like us. Let us become divine for His sake, since for us He became man. He assumed the worse that He might give us the better. He became poor that by His poverty we might become rich. He accepted the form of a servant that we might win back our freedom. He came down that we might be lifted up. He was tempted that through Him we might conquer. He was dishonored that He might glorify us. He died that He might save us. He ascended that He might draw us, who were thrown down through the fall of sin, to Himself. Let us give all, offer all, to Him Who gave Himself as a ransom and reconciliation for us. We needed an incarnate God, a God put to death, that we might live. We were put to death together with Him that we might be

CHAPTER NINE

cleansed. We rose again with Him because we were put to death with Him. We were glorified with Him because we rose again with Him. A few drops of Blood recreate the whole universe!

What reason can be given why the Blood of the Only-begotten should be pleasing to the Father? For He did not accept even Isaac when he was offered by his father, but He gave a substitute for the sacrifice, a lamb to take the place of the rational victim. Is it not clear that the Father accepts the sacrifice, not because he demanded or needed it, but because this was part of the divine economy, since man had to be sanctified by the humanity of God; so that He might rescue us by overcoming the tyrant by force, and bring us back to Himself through the mediation of the Son, Who carried out this divine plan to the honor of the Father, to Whom He clearly delivers up all things.

> **St. Gregory the Theologian**
> from the *Second Theological Oration*

The body of the Word, then, being a real human body, in spite of its having been uniquely formed from a virgin, was of itself mortal and, like other bodies, liable to death. But the indwelling of the Word loosed it from this natural liability, so that corruption could not touch it. Thus it happened that two opposite marvels took place at once: the death of all was consummated in the Lord's body; yet, because the Word was in it, death and corruption were in the same act utterly abolished.

> **St. Athanasius the Great**
> from *On the Incarnation*

LOVE STRONGER THAN DEATH

Special Study

Great and Holy Saturday

Originally, the Feast of Pascha (Easter) was celebrated on one day, Sunday. Over time, however, as the services became more elaborate, the celebration stretched out over three days to comprise the present complex of services of Holy Friday, Saturday, and Pascha itself. At the heart of this liturgical complex is Great and Holy Saturday.

The tone of Great and Holy Saturday is set during Vespers, which is sung on Friday afternoon. This service commemorates the taking down of Christ from the Cross and His entombment. For the first time during the Paschal cycle, we sing "The Noble Joseph": "The Noble Joseph, taking down Thy most pure Body from the Tree, wrapped it in clean linen with sweet spices, and he laid it in a new tomb" (*The Lenten Triodion*).

At Matins, usually sung on Friday evening, the Church gathers around the tomb of Christ, in which is placed the winding sheet or *epitaphios*. The heart of the Matins service is the singing of the *Praises* at the tomb. The Praises consist of short hymns sung alternately with the verses of Psalm 118[119]. These hymns develop two themes that recur throughout the next two days.

CHAPTER NINE

First of all, the hymns are a meditation upon the great condescension of God toward us. We are called to reflect upon the fact that the Creator and Life of all has tasted death to bring us salvation:

> O Life, how canst Thou die? How canst Thou dwell in a tomb? Yet Thou dost destroy death's kingdom and raise the dead from hell.

> O Jesus, King of all, Who hast set measures to the earth, Thou dost go this day to dwell in a narrow grave, raising up the dead from the tombs.

The second theme developed is the descent of Christ into hades itself to release all those held captive. When the Lord gave up His spirit on the Cross, His most pure soul descended into the kingdom of death itself to destroy its power:

> All devouring hell received within himself the Rock of Life, and cast forth all the dead that he had swallowed since the beginning of the world.

> How great the joy, how full the gladness, that Thou hast brought to those in hell, shining as lightning in its gloomy depths.

This theme is further developed during the vesperal Liturgy sung on Saturday afternoon. Here, hell itself testifies to the power of Christ:

> Today hell groans and cries aloud: "My dominion has been swallowed up; the Shepherd has been crucified, and He has raised Adam. I am deprived of those whom once I ruled; in my strength I devoured them, but now I have cast them forth. He Who was

crucified has emptied the tombs; the power of death has no more strength." Glory to Thy Cross, O Lord, and to Thy Resurrection.

To this, the vesperal Liturgy adds the theme of the "Sabbath Rest." We know from the Gospels that our Lord was taken down from the Cross so that He could be buried before the Sabbath began at sunset on Friday. Thus, Christ remained in the tomb during the Sabbath. The hymnographer develops this in a beautiful way:

> Moses the great mystically prefigured this present day, saying: "And God blessed the seventh day." For this is that blessed Sabbath, this is the day of rest, on which the Only-begotten Son of God rested from all His works. Suffering death in accordance with the plan of salvation, He kept the Sabbath in the flesh; and returning once again to what He was, through His Resurrection He has granted us eternal life, for He alone is good and loves mankind.

The Book of Genesis tells us that upon completing the creation of the world on the sixth day, God rested on the seventh. The seventh day represents the fulfillment of the present creation. When Christ descended to death to keep the Sabbath, the created order reached its fulfillment. When He arose from the dead He inaugurated a new order, for He arose not on the first day of a new cycle, but on the Eighth Day, the Day of the New Creation that knows no end.

CHAPTER NINE

Reflection

1. What is the essence of sin?

2. Why does love in our world necessitate sacrifice and suffering?

3. What was necessary to destroy the consequences of man's disobedience?

4. Did Jesus have a human will?

5. What is the significance of Jesus' prayer in the Garden of Gethsemane?

6. Why did St. Gregory the Theologian say we needed "a God put to death"?

7. What happened to the kingdom of death when Christ died?

8. What is the significance of the fact that Christ was in the tomb and in hades during the Sabbath?

9. Did Christ arise in His body, or was it merely a "spiritual" resurrection?

10. What happened to Christ's human nature when He ascended to the right hand of the Father?

Part Two

The Life in Christ

Chapter Ten

The Birth and Mission of the Church

The Church is the historical Body of Christ, Whose mission is to manifest Christ's loving presence to the whole world.

Before his passion, Christ promised His Disciples that He would not leave them comfortless (John 14:18). He promised to send the Holy Spirit, Who would teach the Disciples all things and bring to remembrance all the things which Jesus had taught (John 14:26). It is the Holy Spirit Who unites us with the risen and ascended Christ. Christianity is, therefore, not simply a philosophy of life or a set of rules to follow; it is a living relationship with Christ Himself in the Holy Spirit. This relationship is the life of the Church.

Our holy Fathers teach us that the persons of the Trinity always work together in concert. In particular, the Son and the Spirit complement one another as they accomplish the will of the Father. That is why St. Irenaios referred to Them as "the two hands of God." God spoke the world into existence (Psalm 32[33]:6), and the Spirit hovered over the face of the waters (Genesis 1:3). God created man in His own Image

CHAPTER TEN

(Genesis 1:27), and by His Spirit breathed into man the breath of life (Genesis 2:7).

When, for the salvation of mankind, the Word of God assumed our human nature, it was the Holy Spirit Who came upon the Most Pure Virgin and effected the Incarnation (Luke 1:35). When our Lord was ready to begin His ministry, it was the Holy Spirit, in the form of a dove, Who descended upon Him after His Baptism and anointed Him to be the Messiah of Israel (Mark 1:10). Thus it was that when the Holy Spirit descended upon the Disciples in the Upper Room on the Day of Pentecost, they ceased to be mere followers of Christ and became the Church, the very Body of Christ (Acts 2).

In the Nicene Creed we do not say that we believe *that* there is one, holy, catholic, and apostolic Church. We say that we believe *in* the Church. The Church is an object of faith. This is so because She is Christ's Body, animated by the Holy Spirit. The Apostle Paul wrote that the Church is *the fullness of Him that filleth all in all* (Ephesians 1:23).

We may not think of the Church as simply a religious organization. Jesus did not promise us an organization; He promised to build His Church, which would withstand the gates of hell (Matthew 16:18). Nevertheless, we should not make the opposite mistake of thinking of the Church as something so "spiritual" that She has no real existence in the world. The Church is not now and never has been "invisible."

We confess that the Church is "apostolic." In doing so, we are making definite claims about Her origin, Her

THE BIRTH AND MISSION OF THE CHURCH

life, and Her mission in the world. There are two dimensions to the apostolic nature of the Church. On the one hand, the Church is an historical entity, a visible human community which dates from the time of the Apostles. We shall refer to this as the "horizontal dimension." On the other hand, the Church is an image of the kingdom of heaven; indeed, She is our participation in the heavenly realities. We shall refer to this as the "vertical dimension." Both of these dimensions are essential to the being of the Church. Without *both* aspects, no group of Christians can be called "the Church." In this chapter, we shall focus on the horizontal dimension. In Chapter Eleven, we shall focus on the vertical dimension.

There are four aspects to the horizontal dimension of the Church's life. First of all, the Church is an entity which exists in history. When our Lord became incarnate, He assumed human nature in its entirety. Yet, because humanity does not exist in the abstract, He became a single, concrete human being. He existed in space and time. So, when we say that the Church embraces the totality of the kingdom of heaven, we do not imply that She is "invisible."

Of course, the Church is not limited to Her visible, historical face any more than Christ is limited to His visible, human nature. Yet, Christ did have a visible, human nature that one could see and touch (1 John 1:1). So, too, the Church has a concrete, visible nature. She is the historical apostolic community, made up of real people, and not merely someone's idea of a "perfect" society.

CHAPTER TEN

Second, the Church is founded precisely upon the historical Apostles of Christ. Our Lord said to Peter, *and I say also unto thee, that thou art Peter, and upon this rock I will build My Church; and the gates of hell shall not prevail against it* (Matthew 16:18). Furthermore, it was to Peter, and later to the other Apostles, that Christ gave the keys to the kingdom of heaven and the authority to remit sins: *and I will give unto thee the keys of the kingdom of heaven: and whatsoever thou shalt bind on earth shall be bound in heaven: and whatsoever thou shalt loose on earth shall be loosed in heaven* (Matthew 6:19). *Whosoever sins ye remit, they are remitted unto them; and whosoever sins ye retain, they are retained* (John 20:23).

These words were not spoken to all of Jesus' followers, but to those whom He had called to Himself to be His Apostles. Thus, the Apostle Paul, who was called by the risen Christ on the road to Damascus, says that the Church is built upon *the foundation of the Apostles and prophets, Jesus Christ Himself being the chief corner stone* (Ephesians 2:20).

Because of this, the visible unity of the Church throughout history is expressed in terms of continuity with the Apostles. St. Clement, third Bishop of Rome, wrote in the year A.D. 96:

> Our Apostles also knew through our Lord Jesus Christ that there would be strife over the title of bishop. For this cause, therefore, since they had received perfect foreknowledge, they appointed those who have been already mentioned and afterwards added the codicil that if they should fall asleep,

THE BIRTH AND MISSION OF THE CHURCH

other approved men should succeed to their ministry (*First Epistle of Clement*).

Legitimate authority within the Church is always derived from direct historical succession from the original Apostles. This is called *apostolic succession*. Apostolic succession refers to the historical continuity of a given Church with the original Church in Jerusalem. Succession is traced through the line of bishops because the bishop is the sacramental head of the local Church. In the second century, St. Irenaios of Lyons wrote to combat heretics who claimed to have received "secret knowledge" passed on from the Apostles. He argued that in each place where the Church has been established, the historical links with the Apostles are clearly seen:

> Those who wish to see the truth can observe in every Church the tradition of the Apostles made manifest in the whole world. We can enumerate those who were appointed bishops in the Churches by the Apostles, and their successors down to our own day. They never taught and never knew of such absurdities as those heretics produce (*Against Heresies*).

What has the Church taught about Christ throughout the centuries? Simply look at what the Church's bishops have taught. In the succession of bishops we see the continuity of the Church's faith and life.

This brings us to the third aspect of the Church's apostolic nature: as the inheritor of apostolic authority, the Church must be faithful to apostolic doctrine. The Church is not free to reinvent Her teaching in order to

CHAPTER TEN

get in line with the times. The teaching of the Church must always be the teaching of the Apostles, nothing more and certainly nothing less. In a letter to the English Non-Jurors in 1718, the Orthodox Patriarchs wrote,

> We preserve the Doctrine of the Lord uncorrupted, and firmly adhere to the Faith He delivered to us, and keep it free from blemish and diminution, as a royal treasure, and a monument of great price, neither adding anything nor taking anything from it (quoted in Ware, *The Orthodox Church*, p. 204).

Formal historical links with the Apostles are not enough if apostolic faith is not also preserved. The Church of Rome has an unbroken historical link with the apostolic Church; but, unfortunately, Rome has departed from the apostolic faith on several key issues. This is why the See of Rome has not been in communion with the apostolic Church since the eleventh century.

Fourth, the apostolic nature of the Church means that the Church has a mission to perform in the world. The word *Apostle* means "one who is sent forth with a message." Before His Ascension, Christ told His Disciples:

> *Go ye therefore, and teach all nations, baptizing them in the name of the Father, and of the Son, and of the Holy Spirit, teaching them to observe all things whatsoever I have commanded you: and, lo, I am with you always, even unto the end of the world* (Matthew 28:19-20).

This command was given to the Church as a whole, and it applies to us today every bit as much as it applied to the Apostles in the first century. As members of the apostolic Church of Christ, we have a mission to proclaim the Good News (Gospel) of God's love to the world and to bring the world into the saving embrace of the Church. Thus, the Church is, by definition, a missionary and evangelistic society.

Inasmuch as the Church is the historical Body of Christ, She lives in history. She has an identifiable historical link with the past and an ongoing mission to the world around her. Christianity is not a "private religion." It is a life which can be lived only in communion, for it is nothing less than an earthly participation of the communal life of the Holy Trinity. The Church is not something extra added onto our personal faith; She is the foundation of our faith, our only true spiritual home.

Every day we celebrate the memory of various Saints. These Saints are our ancestors in the faith, our link with the Apostles. To remember the Saints is to affirm the reality of the Church and our place in Her life. It is to confess in a very practical way that we truly believe in one, apostolic Church.

THE FATHERS SPEAK

> The Apostles received the Gospel for us from the Lord Jesus Christ; Jesus the Christ was sent from God. Thus Christ is from God, the Apostles from the Christ: in both cases the process was orderly, and derived from the will of God. The Apostles received their in-

CHAPTER TEN

structions; they were filled with conviction through the Resurrection of our Lord Jesus Christ, and with faith by the Word of God; and they went out full of confidence in the Holy Spirit, preaching the Gospel that the kingdom of God was about to come. They preached in country and town, and appointed their first-fruits, after testing them by the Spirit, to be bishops and deacons of those who were going to believe. And this was no novelty, for indeed a long time ago the Scripture had mentioned bishops and deacons; for there is somewhere this passage: "I will set up their bishops in righteousness and their deacons in faith."

St. Clement of Rome
from *The First Epistle of Clement*
The Early Christian Fathers

By "knowledge of the truth" we mean: the teaching of the Apostles; the order of the Church as established from the earliest times throughout the world, the distinctive stamp of the Body of Christ, preserved through the episcopal succession. For to the bishops the Apostles committed the care of the Church which is in each place, which has come down to our own time, safeguarded without any written documents: by the most complete exposition which admits neither increase or diminution; the reading of the Scriptures without falsification, and consistent and careful exposition of them, avoiding temerity and blasphemy; and the special gift of love, which is more precious than knowledge, more glorious than prophecy, surpassing all other spiritual gifts.

St. Irenaios of Lyons
from *Against Heresies*

THE BIRTH AND MISSION OF THE CHURCH
Special Study
Missions and Evangelism

From Her birth on the Day of Pentecost to the present, the Church has had one mission in the world: to bring mankind back into communion with the All-holy Trinity. The Church is, by definition, a missionary and evangelistic society. Her task is to proclaim to the world the Good News that Christ has come to reconcile man to God and, in so doing, to unite mankind to Christ through Her sacramental life.

After receiving the Holy Spirit on the Day of Pentecost, the Apostles spread the Gospel throughout the known world. St. Peter focused his attention on proclaiming the Good News to the Jews, founding the Church in Antioch and helping to found the Church in Rome. St. Paul was called by God to preach primarily to the Gentiles. His extensive missionary journeys are recorded in the Book of Acts. According to ancient tradition, St. Joseph of Arimathea preached as far west as Britain, St. Thomas spread the Gospel to India, and St. Mark founded the Church in Egypt.

We must remember that this tremendous growth in the early years of the Church took place when Christianity was illegal. Even amidst persecution, the early Christians found the courage not only to share their faith with their neighbors but even to travel to distant

CHAPTER TEN

lands to preach the Good News. They understood well the words of the Savior:

> *Ye are the light of the world. A city that is set on a hill cannot be hid. Neither do men light a candle, and put it under a bushel, but on a candlestick; and it giveth light unto all that are in the house. Let your light so shine before men, that they may see your good works, and glorify your Father Who is in heaven* (Matthew 5:14-16).

Since the era of the Apostles, the Church has been blessed by many missionary Saints. Perhaps the most famous are Ss. Cyril and Methodius, the Enlighteners of the Slavs. In the latter half of the ninth century, these two brothers from Thessalonica invented an alphabet for use by the Moravian Slavs. They translated selections of the Gospels and the Church Office into Slavonic, thus enabling the Slavs to hear the Good News of Christ and to worship Him in their own language.

Not all missionaries, however, went off to foreign countries to sow the Gospel. Many were "home missionaries," preaching and teaching to their own people. Such was St. Cosmas the Aitolian (18th c.), who went about Greece during the Turkish occupation, calling his people back to God. St. Cosmas was responsible, in part, for a great national awakening.

Orthodox Christians in North America are especially blessed by the intercessions of several missionary Saints. St. Herman of Alaska was part of the original Russian Mission to Alaska in 1794. St. Innocent originally came to Alaska as a married priest. After the death of his wife, he returned as a bishop, becoming the first Orthodox hierarch to set foot on North American soil. Later, as Metropolitan of Moscow, he was instrumental in advancing the missionary efforts of the Russian Orthodox Church.

The Church is commanded by our Lord to be a witness of Christ *in Jerusalem, and in all Judea, and in Samaria, and unto the uttermost part of the earth* (Acts 1:8). That is, we are to proclaim the Good News to our local city, state, nation, and, ultimately, to the whole world.

This command is for each and every Orthodox Christian, not just the clergy. All of us are called to bear witness to the light that is within us. All are called to be missionaries to our local communities by living pious lives, by inviting others to Church with us, and by assisting our parishes in local outreach ministries.

Each of us also has a responsibility to proclaim the Gospel on a wider scale. We do this by providing money and materials for missionaries and by volunteering for special missions projects. Currently, Orthodox Christians in America are supporting mission efforts in Haiti, Indonesia, Korea, the Philippines, and Africa. Literally thousands of people around the world are hearing the Gospel and are being united to Christ's Holy Church through these efforts.

Ask your parish priest how you can become a missionary to your local area and how you can support the Church's wider mission efforts. You can also contact the Orthodox Christian Mission Center, P.O. Box 4139, St. Augustine, Florida, 32085-4319 for information.

CHAPTER TEN
Reflection

1. What is meant by the phrase, *the two hands of God*?

2. When was the Church "born"?

3. Why is the Church an object of faith?

4. Why is the historical aspect of the Church important?

5. To which Apostle did Christ give the keys of the kingdom of heaven?

6. What did Christ promise about the endurance of the Church?

7. What is apostolic succession?

8. How is apostolic succession traced?

9. Are the bishops free to make up their own doctrines and teachings?

10. In what ways can you serve as a missionary to your local community?

Chapter Eleven
The Structure of the Church

The Church is composed of the local bishop, presbyters, deacons, and laity, gathered around the Holy Table, reflecting here on earth the unity and harmony of the All-holy Trinity.

The Apostle Peter, to whom the Lord entrusted the keys to the kingdom of heaven, compared the Church to a spiritual house: *Ye also, as living stones, are built up a spiritual house, a holy priesthood, to offer up spiritual sacrifices, acceptable to God by Jesus Christ* (1 Peter 2:5). Just as a physical house is built according to a specific plan and has a definite structure, so does the spiritual house that is the Church.

Every building must have a blueprint and building materials that are appropriate to it. One could not build a skyscraper with the blueprints for a Cape Cod house. Nor could one build a skyscraper with pine two-by-fours; they could never support the weight of the building. In the same way, the Church must be designed and built with that which is appropriate to Her inner nature.

CHAPTER ELEVEN

Regarding the Church's blueprint, Archimandrite Vasileios notes,

> If the Lord had wanted a merely administrative unity, with no further implications in terms of life and mystery, He would have provided as an image of the Church's unity the Roman Empire, saying, "Father, I desire that the faithful may be united as the Roman Empire is united" (*Hymn of Entry*, p. 47).

Our Lord, however, did not do this. Before His Ascension to heaven, He prayed not that His Disciples would attain to the unity of any worldly organization but to that of the Holy Trinity:

> *That they all may be one; as Thou, Father, art in Me, and I in Thee, that they also may be one in Us; that the world may believe that Thou hast sent Me. And the glory which Thou gavest Me I have given them; that they may be one, even as We are one: I in them and Thou in Me, that they may be made perfect in one; and that the world may know that Thou hast sent Me, and hast loved them, as Thou hast loved Me* (John 17:21-23).

The Church is, therefore, an act of communion with God. She is mankind's participation in and through Christ in the eternal relationship of love among the Father, Son, and Holy Spirit: *that they may be one, even as We are one.* Commenting on the communal nature of the Church, Metropolitan John (Zizioulas) writes:

> For the Church to present this way of existence, she must herself be an image of the way in which God exists. Her entire structure, her ministries etc. must express this way of existence (*Being as Communion*, p. 15).

THE STRUCTURE OF THE CHURCH

The structure of the Church, therefore, is a reflection of Her heavenly archetype, the Holy Trinity. In the Book of Acts we read that the first Christians *continued steadfastly in the Apostles' doctrine and fellowship, and in the breaking of the Bread and the prayers* (Acts 2:42). At the very outset of the Christian era, then, we find the Church gathered around the Table of Her Lord for "the breaking of the Bread." Because the Church is first and foremost a eucharistic community, it is in the Eucharist that the Trinitarian structure of the Church is most clearly manifest.

At these gatherings, someone had to preside; someone had to repeat the words of Christ, offer prayers for the community, and distribute the Gifts. Obviously, the Apostles themselves would have led these initial services, but what about the leadership in the various local Churches? We know from the New Testament that the Apostles appointed bishops, presbyters, and deacons to lead the local communities. The roles that these persons played in the life of the Church were defined in the eucharistic gathering.

In the New Testament the terms *bishop* and *presbyter* are used interchangeably. This does not mean, however, that the specific offices themselves were interchangeable. It simply means that the terminology had not been precisely defined. This makes perfect sense when we consider that the bishop is himself a presbyter, the *presiding* presbyter.

St. Clement, the third Bishop of Rome, wrote a very important letter to the Church in Corinth around the year A.D. 96. In it, he also used bishop and presbyter interchangeably, yet it is perfectly clear from the letter that he had a specific Church structure in mind:

> He commanded us to celebrate sacrifices and services, and that it should not be thoughtlessly or disorderly, but at fixed times and hours. He has Himself fixed by His supreme will the places and persons whom He desires for these celebrations, in order that all things may be done piously according to His good pleasure, and be acceptable to His will. . . . For to the high priest his proper ministrations are allotted, and to the priests the proper place has been appointed, and on levites their proper services have been imposed. The layman is bound by the ordinances for the laity (*First Epistle of Clement*).

Here St. Clement used the Old Testament imagery of the high priest, priests, and levites to represent the bishop, presbyters, and deacons.

Notice also that St. Clement considered the laity to be a specific order of the Church. The importance of the laity in the life of the Church is stressed in canon law by the fact that priests are forbidden from celebrating the Liturgy alone. There must be at least one other person present to represent the People of God.

St. Irenaios of Lyons, writing around the year A.D. 180, also used bishop and presbyter interchangeably. As with St. Clement, however, it is perfectly clear that he was thinking of a specific structure. Although he spoke of the presbyters as having their succession from the Apostles, when providing a list for the apostolic succession of the Church of Rome he gave a list of single names, one bishop succeeding another: Linus, Anacle-

THE STRUCTURE OF THE CHURCH

tus, Clement (mentioned above), Euarestus, Alexander, Sixtus, Telesphorus, Hyginus, Pius, Anicetus, Sotor, and Eleutherus. Irenaios may have used the terms interchangeably, but there is no doubt that he knew of only one bishop in a local Church at one time.

In the second century, there was one writer, however, who did use bishop and presbyter consistently, and his usage eventually became the standard throughout the Church. St. Ignatius became Bishop of Antioch, the city where the Disciples were first called "Christians," sometime in the late 70's of the first century. Around the year A.D. 107 he was arrested and taken to Rome to be martyred. On his way he wrote seven important letters to various Churches.

St. Ignatius' primary concern was the unity of the Church. Just as the Father is the principle of unity within the Holy Trinity, so the bishop is the center of the visible unity of the Church on earth:

> I advise you, be eager to act always in godly concord; with the bishop presiding as the counterpart of God, the presbyters as the counterpart of the council of the Apostles, and the deacons (most dear to me) who have been entrusted with a service under Jesus Christ, Who was with the Father before all ages and appeared at the end of time.... Let there be nothing among you which will have power to divide you, but be united with the bishop and with those who preside, for an example and instruction in incorruptibility (*Epistle to the Magnesians*).

St. Ignatius' terminology eventually became the standard terminology for the whole Church. Thus, the

CHAPTER ELEVEN

local Church is comprised of one bishop, who is the first and presiding presbyter, the college of presbyters, the deacons, and the laity — the People of God.

In modern parish life, however, there is usually only one presbyter. The bishop is head of a large diocese and may only visit a given parish once every couple of years. How did this come about, and how does the modern structure of the Church reflect the ancient practice?

In the early years, Christianity was primarily an urban phenomenon. There was only one Church in a given city. As more and more people in outlying areas responded to the Gospel, however, it became impossible for all of the people in a given area to meet at one place at one time for the Eucharist.

In North Africa the problem was solved by simply duplicating the existing Church structure in every little village. Thus, communities with less than 25 people could end up with a bishop, a council of presbyters, and deacons. This, however, proved very impractical, and the practice did not last long.

Elsewhere, the bishop of the local Church delegated presbyters and deacons to go to the various outlying areas and villages and minister there, creating what we call today "parishes." The grouping of parishes around a local Church is now called a "diocese."

In modern practice, then, the local Church is the diocese, comprised of its bishop, all of the presbyters (who are usually appointed as pastors of individual parishes), all of the deacons (also attached to individual parishes), and all of the faithful. This situation is the

THE STRUCTURE OF THE CHURCH

product of the Church's tremendous growth. It allows for expansion of the Church yet at the same time preserves Her basic Trinitarian structure.

Because of this Trinitarian structure, each local Church is "catholic." That is, She is whole and complete, lacking nothing for the salvation of Her members. The many Churches throughout the world are united by an identical faith and sacramental life and by the communion of their bishops.

Churches in a given area, usually but not always coinciding with national borders, are grouped together. Their bishops meet together regularly in meetings called "synods." The largest synod by far is the Synod of the Church of Russia, chaired by the Patriarch of Moscow. The Synod of the Church of Cyprus, on the other hand, is quite small by comparison.

Size, however, has nothing to do with holiness. The dioceses (local Churches) that make up the Church of Cyprus are no less Orthodox, no less possessed of the promises of Christ, than the dioceses which make up the Church of Russia. Ultimately, it is the presence of Christ Himself in the Church that makes each and every local Church His Body, *the fullness of Him that filleth all in all.*

CHAPTER ELEVEN
THE FATHERS SPEAK

Let no one do anything that pertains to the Church apart from the bishop. Let that be considered a valid Eucharist which is under the bishop or one whom he has delegated. Wherever the bishop shall appear, there let the people be; just as wherever Christ Jesus may be, there is the catholic Church.

Take great care to keep one Eucharist. For there is one Flesh of our Lord Jesus Christ and one Cup to unite us by His Blood; one sanctuary, as there is one bishop, together with the presbytery and the deacons, my fellow-servants. Thus all your acts may be done according to God's will.

St. Ignatius of Antioch
from the *Epistles*
The Early Christian Fathers

For where the Church is, there is the Spirit of God; and where the Spirit of God is, there is the Church and every kind of grace. The Spirit is truth. Therefore those who have no share in the Spirit are not nourished and given life at their mother's breast, nor do they enjoy the sparkling fountain that issues from the Body of Christ.

St. Irenaios of Lyons
from *Against Heresies*
The Early Christian Fathers

THE STRUCTURE OF THE CHURCH

Special Study

Ecumenical Councils

During the early years of the Church, when a dispute arose concerning whether or not gentile converts should be circumcised, the Apostles met together in Jerusalem to resolve the issue (cf. Acts 15). This council set the precedent for all future gatherings of the Church's leaders.

As the Church grew and spread throughout the Roman Empire, it became necessary for the bishops of Churches in a given area to meet together on a regular basis to address issues of common concern. Apostolic Canon 34 provides for the creation of a regional synod. The bishops of a given area were to gather together twice a year. The meetings were to be chaired by the bishop of the major city in the area, the *metropolis*. The bishop of this city became known as the *metropolitan*.

Each bishop was responsible for the governance of his Church. Issues of common concern, however, were brought before the regional synod and decided by all of the bishops. The metropolitan did not "rule" the synod, but he did have veto power over the synod's decisions. Just as nothing within a given Church could be done without the bishop's approval, so nothing could be done in a region that affected more than one Church without the approval of the metropolitan. The metropolitan, then, served as the principle of unity within the synod.

CHAPTER ELEVEN

Some issues, however, such as doctrinal questions, involved more than the Churches of a particular region. For this reason, larger gatherings of bishops were called to deal with issues pertaining to the universal Church. The largest and most important of these gatherings are called the Ecumenical Councils.

The Ecumenical Councils were originally convened by the Roman Emperor and presided over by a senior bishop. The Orthodox Church recognizes seven councils as being Ecumenical:

> **Nicea I** (A.D. 325) This Council was called to deal with the heresy of Arianism—the teaching that the Word and Son of God is a created being. The first part of the Nicene Creed was drafted here. The hero of Nicea I was St. Athanasius of Alexandria, whose theology was decisive even though, as a deacon at the time, he could not vote.
>
> **Constantinople I** (A.D. 381) This Council expanded and completed the Nicene Creed and affirmed the divinity of the Holy Spirit. The theology of the Cappadocian Fathers—St. Basil the Great, St. Gregory the Theologian, and St. Gregory of Nyssa—was particularly influential here.
>
> **Ephesus** (A.D. 431) This Council condemned the teachings of Patriarch Nestorius of Constantinople, who refused to accept the unity of humanity and divinity in the person of Christ and who refused to call the Virgin Mary *Theotokos*. St. Cyril, Archbishop of Alexandria, was the hero of this Council.

THE STRUCTURE OF THE CHURCH

Chalcedon (A.D. 451) This Council was called to combat the opposite heresy of Nestorianism: Monophysitism. According to the Monophysites, Christ's divine nature swallowed up His human nature, leaving Him with only one nature. The bishops accepted the *Tome* of Pope St. Leo the Great along with the theology of St. Cyril of Alexandria as the standard of Orthodox thought concerning the person of Christ. The Council decreed that in Christ the divine and human natures exist without "mixture, confusion, division, or separation."

Constantinople II (A.D. 553) This Council further elaborated on the decisions of the Council of Chalcedon. In addition, some of the teachings of Origen of Alexandria, such as the pre-existence of souls, were condemned.

Constantinople III (A.D. 681) This Council condemned the heresy of Monothelitism, which held that Christ had only one will. The bishops affirmed that Christ has a perfect human will as well as a perfect divine will, thus affirming His full humanity. Pope Honorius of Rome was condemned as a heretic for his support of the Monothelites.

Quinisext (A.D. 692) This Council, also called the Council in Trullo, is considered a continuation of the Fifth and Sixth Councils and not a separate Council unto itself. Among other things, it reaffirmed the condemnation of the teachings of Origen.

CHAPTER ELEVEN

Nicea II (A.D. 787) This Council was called to decide the appropriateness of using icons in the Church. The bishops decreed that the veneration (not worship) of icons was necessary to preserve a proper understanding of the Incarnation.

It is important to note that not all large councils are considered Ecumenical Councils. We often speak of Ecumenical Councils as being "infallible," but there was no guarantee at the beginning of any of these Councils that they would be considered infallible. Only after the decisions of a Council have been received by the consciousness of the whole Church can it be called Ecumenical and infallible.

When the bishops meet together in council, they do not invent new doctrines. Rather, their job is to express the mind and life of the Church. A specific situation, such as the challenge of a new heresy, may necessitate the development of the Church's vocabulary or a change in the way the Church expresses a particular idea. Nevertheless, it is the duty of the bishops to elaborate upon what the Church has always believed and experienced, not to invent new teachings.

When, however, bishops in council did deviate from *the faith once delivered* and made decrees contrary to the faith and life of the Church, the Body of the Church throughout the world rejected the decisions. A council held in Ephesus in 449 had a greater number of bishops in attendance than many Ecumenical Councils, yet its decisions were rejected by the Church at large. It has gone down in history as the "Robber Council."

THE STRUCTURE OF THE CHURCH

The purpose of a council, whether a regular meeting of a regional synod or a gathering of all of the world's bishops, is to express the mind and heart of the Church as a whole. No single bishop, not even a patriarch, can claim exclusive rights to the Holy Spirit. The bishops are answerable to the whole Church for their decisions.

It is this conciliar process, reflecting the conciliar nature of the All-holy Trinity, which is the supreme expression of authority within the Church. It is for this reason that the Church cannot and will not accept the claims of the Bishop of Rome to be infallible and to rule over the entire Church.

CHAPTER ELEVEN
Reflection

1. In what way is the Church like a building?

2. What is the archetype for the structure of the Church?

3. The Church is first and foremost what kind of community?

4. What Church offices are mentioned in the New Testament?

5. What Old Testament offices did St. Clement use to represent the New Testament offices?

6. Who was the first Church Father to use the terms *bishop*, *presbyter*, and *deacon* in exactly the same way we do today?

7. Who serves as the principle of unity within the local Church?

8. Are the laity any less important that the bishop or presbyters?

9. What do we call the gathering of bishops in a particular region?

10. What is the purpose of a Church council?

Chapter Twelve
Holy Baptism

In Holy Baptism our fallen nature is put to death, and we are raised from the water, purified from sin, to live a new life united with Christ our God.

The last commandment that Christ gave to His Disciples before His Ascension to heaven was:

Go ye therefore, and teach all nations, baptizing them in the name of the Father, and of the Son, and of the Holy Spirit: Teaching them to observe all things whatsoever I have commanded you: and, lo, I am with you always, even unto the end of the world (Matthew 28:19-20).

Our Lord made Baptism a central element of the Christian Faith: *He that believeth and is baptized shall be saved* (Mark 16:16). This underscores the fact that Christianity is not merely a philosophy or a set of beliefs, but a life to be lived. Baptism is our entrance into this life.

Before we discuss Baptism in detail, however, a few words about the sacraments in general are in order. First of all, we should note that the Greek word for "sacrament" is *mysterion*, from which we get the word *mystery*. In the Orthodox Church, the sacraments are usually referred to as the mysteries.

CHAPTER TWELVE

It is often said that a sacrament is "an outward sign of an invisible grace." But what exactly do we mean by grace, and how is this communicated to us through the mysteries?

The Church teaches that grace is more than God's "good favor" toward man; it is the uncreated energy of God. When God bestows His grace upon man, He is bestowing the gift of Himself. God's inner nature is incommunicable. Created man can never come to know the inner nature of the uncreated God. Nevertheless, God truly communicates His life to man. When man encounters the grace of God, he encounters God Himself.

Because man is a physical being, God communicates His grace to man through physical means. Created matter becomes the vehicle through which God's presence reaches into our lives. The mysteries, therefore, are our way of participating in the life of the Holy Trinity, which Christ came to give to mankind.

Baptism is the first of the mysteries, our introduction into the divine life. In Holy Baptism, past sins are remitted, our fallen nature is put to death, and we are raised to *walk in newness of life* (Romans 6:4) in the likeness of the Son of God. For this reason the baptismal pool is known as the *tomb* and the *womb*.

Baptism begins with the exorcism of the candidate and his renunciation of Satan. While speaking with His Disciples our Lord made a very disturbing comment: *He that is not with Me is against Me; and he that gathereth not with Me scattereth abroad* (Matthew 12:30). There are only two choices in life: God or Satan. To accept one is to reject the other.

The Scriptures describe Satan as *the god of this world* (2 Corinthians 4:4) and as *a roaring lion, which walketh about, seeking whom he may devour* (1 Peter 5:8). From the Fall of Adam to the coming of Christ, all mankind lay under the sway of Satan. The first step in becoming a Christian is to be freed of the devil's power and to renounce his claim upon our lives. "Dost thou renounce Satan, and all his angels, and all his works, and all his service, and all his pride?"

After the renunciation of Satan, the candidate recites the Symbol of Faith—the Nicene Creed. The Creed was written specifically for use at Baptism and only later was inserted into the Divine Liturgy. This is why, when we sing or recite the Creed at the Liturgy, we say "I believe" rather than "We believe." Each time we do so, we are renewing our personal confession of faith originally made at our Baptism.

Baptism is performed by triple immersion in the name of the Father, and of the Son, and of the Holy Spirit. Baptism cannot take place without the invocation of the All-holy Trinity. St. Nicholas Cabasilas wrote:

> Even though it is by one single act of loving-kindness that the Trinity has saved our race, yet each of the blessed persons is said to have contributed something of His own. It is the Father Who is reconciled, the Son Who reconciles, while the Holy Spirit is bestowed as a gift on those who have become friends (*The Life in Christ*).

CHAPTER TWELVE

The candidate is immersed three times in commemoration of Christ's three-day burial. This underscores the fact that our Baptism is our participation in the death of Christ. In the waters of Baptism our fallen human nature is put to death together with Christ, that we might also rise with Him: *Buried with Him in Baptism, wherein also ye are risen with Him through the faith of the operation of God, Who hath raised Him from the dead* (Colossians 2:12).

We must remember that the operative element here is the power of the death of Christ and not our own effort. St. Cyril of Jerusalem stressed this point:

> O strange and inconceivable thing! We did not really die, we were not really buried, we were not really crucified and raised again, but our imitation was but in a figure, while our salvation is in reality. Christ was actually crucified, and actually buried, and truly rose again; and all these things have been vouchsafed to us, that we, by imitation communicating in His sufferings, might gain salvation in reality (*On the Sacraments*).

This point is also emphasized by the fact that the baptismal formula is in the third person. The priest does not say, "I baptize thee," but, "The Servant of God is baptized." Baptism is not an act that we or even the priest performs, but is an act of God. It is God Who died in the flesh and rose again for our salvation and God Who unites us to Himself through our sacramental participation in His sufferings.

Inasmuch as our fallen nature dies with Christ in Baptism, so are we freed from the Ancestral Sin inherited from our forefather Adam. In the Orthodox Church, the Original Sin is frequently referred to as the Ancestral Sin. Our Holy Fathers did not understand this to mean that we inherit the *guilt* for Adam's transgression. Rather, we inherit an inclination to sin to the point that it is much easier for us to sin than not. Our life is dominated by the passions.

Most of all, however, the Ancestral Sin refers to man's enslavement to corruption and death: *Wherefore, as by one man sin entered into the world, and death by sin; and so death passed upon all men, for that all have sinned* (Romans 5:12). Our enslavement to the passions are but proof of our ultimate bondage to the power of death. St. Paul lamented, *O wretched man that I am! Who shall deliver me from the body of this death* (Romans 7:24)?

We have seen that when Christ died, His most pure soul descended into the depths of hades to destroy the power of death forever. In Baptism, we too descend with Christ so that we might share in His victory:

> *For if we have been planted together in the likeness of His death, we shall be also in the likeness of His Resurrection: Knowing this, that our old man is crucified with Him, that the body of sin might be destroyed, that henceforth we should not serve sin. For he that is dead is freed from sin* (Romans 6:5-7).

In Baptism, then, our fallen nature is put to death and our sins, both Ancestral and actual, are forgiven, as we recite in the Creed: "I confess one Baptism for the remission of sins." We die with Christ, and our sins are forgiven so that we might share in His life. From the water, therefore, we emerge reborn as true children of

CHAPTER TWELVE

our heavenly Father: "At the self-same moment, ye died and were born; and that water of salvation was at once your grave and your mother" (St. Cyril of Jerusalem).

Once a leader of the Jews named Nicodemus came to Christ for spiritual nourishment (John 3:2-21). Our Lord told him, *"Except a man be born again, he cannot see the kingdom of God."* Nicodemus was understandably confused by this strange saying. Then Christ explained, *"Except a man be born of water and of the Spirit, he cannot enter into the kingdom of God. That which is born of the flesh is flesh; and that which is born of the Spirit is spirit."*

Baptism is our birth of water and of the Spirit. All those who have been rightly baptized in the name of the Holy Trinity have been "born again." Once again, we must stress that this new birth is not of our doing, but is the work of God. It is God alone Who bestows the gift of life upon His children who emerge purified from the baptismal waters.

Of course, having been granted new life in Christ, it is up to us to live in accordance with it. Nevertheless, it is God Who first bestows the gift. The "new birth" is the result neither of our efforts nor of any "personal decision for Christ" but is the result of the grace of God imparted to us in the Mystery of Holy Baptism: *But as many as received Him, to them gave He power to become the sons of God, even to them that believe on His name: which were born, not of blood, nor of the will of the flesh, nor of the will of man, but of God* (John 1:12-13).

After Baptism the newly illumined Servant of God is clothed in a white robe—the robe of righteousness. Our nakedness is covered by the righteousness of God as we prepare to lead our new life in communion with the All-holy Trinity: "Grant unto me the robe of light, O most merciful Christ our God, Who clothest Thyself with light as with a garment."

Great, therefore, is the mystery of our salvation, and great are the benefits bestowed upon us in Holy Baptism. We die to a world of sin and death and rise to walk in the immortal life of God Himself. Having emerged from the waters reborn and having been clothed with the garment of salvation, we are ready to receive within us the Holy Spirit—to become the living temples of God.

THE FATHERS SPEAK

It is for us, dearly beloved brothers, for us that these mysteries were celebrated. For by the most sacred bathing of His body the Lord dedicated for us the bath of Baptism, and He also pointed out to us that, after the reception of Baptism, the right of entry into heaven is accessible to us, and the Holy Spirit is given to us.

St. Bede the Venerable
from *Homilies on the Gospels*
Tr. by Martin and Hurst
Cistercian Pub., 1991

CHAPTER TWELVE

As soon as he has thrice emerged from the water after being submerged therein during the invocation of the Trinity, he who has been initiated receives all that he seeks. He is born and receives form by that birth which is of the day which David mentions (Psalm [138] 139:16). He receives the noble seal and possesses all the happiness which he has sought. He who once was darkness becomes light; he who once was nothing now has existence. He enters God's household and is like a son who has been adopted; from the dungeon and utmost slavery he is led to the royal Throne.

So this water destroys the one life and brings the other into the open; it drowns the old man and raises up the new. . . . For this cause we here invoke the Creator, since what takes place here is a beginning of life and a second creation which is far better than the first. The image is delineated more accurately than before, and the statue is molded more clearly according to the divine pattern; wherefore the archetype must needs be the more perfectly set forth.

St. Nicholas Cabasilas
from *The Life in Christ*

We all know that if one baptized in infancy does not believe when he comes to years of discretion, and does not keep himself from lawless desires, then he will have no profit from the gift he received as a baby.

Blessed Augustine
from *On the Due Reward*
The Later Christian Fathers

HOLY BAPTISM

Special Study
The Baptism of Tears

Baptism bestows new life in Christ, but it is up to us to live in accordance with that life. Baptism bestows the forgiveness of sins, but it is up to us to walk in the commandments of Christ. Baptism bestows the robe of righteousness, but it is up to us to preserve that garment unspotted.

All of this is easier said than done, however. As long as we live in this world, the devil, whom we have renounced and spat upon, will oppose our efforts. We all fall and soil our baptismal garments, but God in His infinite wisdom and mercy has provided for the renewal of the grace of Baptism in the "Baptism of Tears," which is the Mystery of Repentance:

> The tears that come after Baptism are greater than Baptism itself, though it may seem rash to say so. Baptism washes off those evils that were previously within us, whereas the sins committed after Baptism are washed away by tears. The Baptism received by us as children we have all defiled, but we cleanse it anew with our tears. If God in His love for mankind had not given us tears, those being saved would be few indeed and hard to find (St. John Climacus, *The Ladder of Divine Ascent*).

In the Mystery of Confession, our Baptism is renewed as we are cleansed of the sins we commit each day. The power to forgive sins was conferred upon the Church by our Lord after His Resurrection:

> *As my Father hath sent Me, even so send I you. And when He had said this, He breathed on them, and saith unto them, "Receive ye the Holy Spirit: Whosesoever sins ye remit, they are remitted unto them; and whosesoever sins ye retain, they are retained "* (John 20:21-23).

When, therefore, we come to Confession, we come not before a mere man, but before our Lord Himself, Who grants forgiveness of sins through His Apostles and their successors: "Behold, my Child, Christ standeth here invisibly receiving thy Confession. . . . Behold His icon before us! I am but a witness bearing testimony before Him of all things that thou sayest unto me."

Frequent Confession is a prerequisite for frequent Communion. We cannot approach the Holy Chalice and partake of the Body and Blood of Christ while our soul is infected with sin and our conscience accuses us. St. Paul warns us, *he that eateth and drinketh unworthily, eateth and drinketh damnation to himself, not discerning the Lord's Body* (1 Corinthians 11:29). St. John Chrysostom adds:

> I would give up my own life rather than grant the reception of the Blood of the Lord unworthily: I would shed my own blood rather than wrongfully grant reception of Blood so awesome (*Homily 82 on Matthew*).

It is important to note here, however, that in the Orthodox Church sin is thought of primarily as a sickness. The emphasis is on healing, rather than on meeting a legalistic requirement or eliminating our guilt feelings. We should, therefore, approach our father confessor as we would our family physician.

When we go to Confession we must tell the priest of our specific sins, but we need not go into detail. We must never implicate or blame another person for our sins, nor may we try to find excuses for our actions. We must lay our sins before our spiritual physician clearly and without elaboration. If he needs more information in order to diagnose and treat our illness, he will ask for it.

It goes without saying that we must always answer the priest fully and truthfully, hiding nothing, for it is not the priest whom we address, but the Lord Himself: "If thou shalt conceal anything from me, thou shalt have the greater sin. Take heed, therefore, lest having come to the Physician, thou depart unhealed."

When we have told our spiritual doctor of our symptoms, he will make his diagnosis. He may prescribe a penance (*epitimia*). This is *not* a punishment. It is a medical treatment designed to cure us of our spiritual ills. We must obey the priest as we would our family doctor and, taking the medicine that he prescribes, receive healing for our souls.

Great is the Mystery of Baptism, and great is the Mystery of Repentance, whereby our Baptism is renewed and the sins that beset us day by day are overcome: *If Thou, LORD, shouldest mark iniquities, O Lord, who shall stand? But there is forgiveness with Thee* (Psalm 129[130]:3-4).

CHAPTER TWELVE

Reflection

1. Why is Baptism necessary for living the Christian life?

2. The sacraments are usually referred to in the Orthodox Church as what?

3. Is grace created or uncreated?

4. What is the first act of the baptismal service?

5. When reciting the Creed in the Liturgy, why do we say "I believe" rather than "We believe"?

6. Why are we immersed three times?

7. How is the baptismal font like a tomb?

8. How is the baptismal font like a womb?

9. How is our Baptism renewed?

10. How ought we think of our father confessor?

Chapter Thirteen
The Seal of the Gift of the Holy Spirit

The Mystery of Chrismation is our personal Pentecost, in which we receive the Holy Spirit and become living temples of the All-holy Trinity.

At the beginning of His ministry, our Lord Jesus Christ accepted Baptism in the Jordan River at the hands of St. John the Forerunner. When He emerged from the water, the Holy Spirit alighted upon Him and anointed Him to be the Christ or Messiah:

> *And Jesus, when He was baptized, went up straightway out of the water: and, lo, the heavens were opened unto Him, and He saw the Spirit of God descending like a dove, and lighting upon Him: And lo a voice from heaven, saying, "This is My beloved Son, in Whom I am well pleased"* (Matthew 3:16-17).

So also, when we emerge from the baptismal waters, cleansed of our sins, we are anointed with Holy Chrism and receive in ourselves the Spirit of the Living God. Chrismation is our personal Pentecost. By virtue of this mystery, we become living temples of God.

CHAPTER THIRTEEN

In the New Testament, the Holy Spirit was conferred upon the newly baptized by the Apostles:

Now when the Apostles which were at Jerusalem heard that Samaria had received the Word of God, they sent unto them Peter and John: who, when they were come down, prayed for them, that they might receive the Holy Spirit: (For as yet He was fallen upon none of them: only they were baptized in the name of the Lord Jesus.) Then laid they their hands on them, and they received the Holy Spirit (Acts 8:15-17).

At some point between the time of the Acts of the Apostles and the second century the method of the mystery was changed from the laying on of hands to anointing with Holy Oil. This change no doubt reflected the way the Apostles perceived the mystery: *But ye have an unction from the Holy One, and ye know all things* (1 John 2:20).

In the New Testament, the conferral of the Holy Spirit was the prerogative of the Apostles. This authority is retained in the Church by their successors, the bishops. In the West, the mystery (called *Confirmation*) could be performed only by bishops. In the East, presbyters perform the anointing, but the Chrism itself must be consecrated by the bishop. In modern practice, the Chrism is consecrated by the Chief Hierarch of the national Church.

Although the effects of Chrismation are manifold, we shall focus on three of the most important effects. First of all, Chrismation bestows upon us the Spirit of Adoption, making us children of God. Second, it is our anointing into the royal priesthood. Third, Chrism is

THE SEAL OF THE GIFT OF THE HOLY SPIRIT

the pledge of our future inheritance of the kingdom of God.

Jesus Christ, the Only-begotten Son and Word of God the Father, descended from heaven and took upon Himself our humanity for one reason: to reconcile man to God and introduce him into the eternal communion of love that is the life of the Holy Trinity. Through Holy Chrism we personally receive the Holy Spirit, Who is the Spirit of Adoption:

> *Even so we, when we were children, were in bondage under the elements of the world: But when the fulness of the time was come, God sent forth His Son, made of a woman, made under the law, to redeem them that were under the law, that we might receive the adoption of sons. And because ye are sons, God hath sent forth the Spirit of His Son into your hearts, crying, "Abba, Father"* (Galatians 4:3-6).

From all eternity the Holy Spirit proceeds from the Father and rests in the Son. When we receive the Holy Spirit He rests upon us, making us like unto the Son of God. *Abba*, incidentally, is an Aramaic term of endearment, often translated into English as "Daddy." In this way, we enter into the intimate relationship of love between the Father and the Son and become co-heirs with Christ in His heavenly inheritance:

> *For as many as are led by the Spirit of God, they are the sons of God. For ye have not received the spirit of bondage again to fear; but ye have received the Spirit of Adoption, whereby we cry, "Abba, Father." The Spirit Himself beareth witness with our spirit, that we are the children of God: And if children, then heirs; heirs of God,*

CHAPTER THIRTEEN

and joint-heirs with Christ; if so be that we suffer with Him, that we may be also glorified together (Romans 8:14-17).

Holy Chrism is, therefore, our introduction into the life of the Holy Trinity. "When Thou wast baptized in the Jordan, the worship of the Trinity was made manifest," we sing at the Feast of the Lord's Baptism. So it is at our Baptism and Chrismation that the Holy Trinity is made manifest in our lives.

In addition to bestowing upon us the adoption as children of God, the Holy Spirit also bestows spiritual power and priestly dignity. Before His Ascension, our Lord commanded the Apostles: *"I send the promise of My Father upon you: but tarry ye in the city of Jerusalem, until ye be endued with power from on high"* (Luke 24:49). This power is the Holy Spirit, Who came upon the Apostles at Pentecost and comes upon us at our Chrismation.

In the Old Testament, the priests of God were anointed with oil after being washed in water and robed with their priestly vestments:

> *And Aaron and his sons thou shalt bring unto the door of the tabernacle of the congregation, and shalt wash them with water. And thou shalt take the garments, and put upon Aaron the coat, and the robe of the ephod, and the ephod, and the breastplate, and gird him with the curious girdle of the ephod: And thou shalt put the mitre upon his head, and put the holy crown upon the mitre. Then shalt thou take the Anointing Oil, and pour it upon his head, and anoint him* (Exodus 29:4-7).

After we are washed and robed, we too receive the priestly anointing for service in God's Church. This is why the Apostle Peter calls the members of the Church a royal priesthood: *But ye are a chosen generation, a royal priesthood, an holy nation, a peculiar people; that ye should show forth the praises of Him Who hath called you out of darkness into His marvellous light* (1 Peter 2:9).

There is only one Priest in the Church—Jesus Christ, the great High Priest of our salvation. However, inasmuch as we are united with Him in Baptism and anointed with the Spirit of His anointing, we all share in His priesthood, that is, His ministry of reconciliation between God and man. The fact that some within the Church are set apart specifically to serve at the altar in no way abrogates the responsibility of *every* member of the Church to share in Christ's work of reconciliation and bring the glorious gift of God's grace to the world.

By virtue of our Chrismation, each of us is endowed by God with spiritual gifts for service within the Church. These gifts are not a principle of individualism and self-sufficiency, but of unity:

> *Now there are diversities of gifts, but the same Spirit. And there are differences of administrations, but the same Lord. And there are diversities of operations, but it is the same God which worketh all in all. But the manifestation of the Spirit is given to every man to profit withal* (1 Corinthians 12:7).

It is important to note that the phrase *royal priesthood* is used in the Scripture only to refer to the Church as a whole, not to individuals. The reason for this is clear: the gifts of the Spirit are the means whereby each member of the Body of Christ contributes to the life of

CHAPTER THIRTEEN

the whole. That which leads to strife and dissension is not of God.

When He, the Spirit of Truth, is come, He will guide you into all truth (John 16:13). Likewise, St. John writes that the Anointing that we receive teaches us all things (1 John 2:27). This does not mean, however, that we as individuals have the capacity to interpret the Scriptures on our own. On the contrary, *no prophecy of the Scripture is of any private interpretation* (1 Peter 1:20). The truth is given to the Church as a body, and it is within that communal fellowship of divine love that we, as unique persons, come to experience and know the truth.

It is, therefore, the Holy Spirit Who equips each of us for our unique role in the Body of the Lord. As the Apostle Paul teaches, we cannot all be hand or all eye. Each of us has our part; each is necessary and unique (cf. 1 Corinthians 12). The Holy Spirit, therefore, unifies us through the multiplicity of gifts, even as the many tongues of fire that descended upon the Apostles on the day of Pentecost unified them and anointed them to be the Church (cf. Acts 2).

Every baptized and chrismated Orthodox Christian, therefore, is a child of God and a priestly minister of His love to the world. We know, however, that this present world is not our true home. *In the world ye shall have tribulation: but be of good cheer; I have overcome the world* (John 16:33). As Christians, we await the return of the One Who has overcome the world and the establishment of His eternal kingdom. Chrismation is our guarantee toward that end.

THE SEAL OF THE GIFT OF THE HOLY SPIRIT

In his Second Epistle to the Corinthians, St. Paul described the Holy Spirit as a "down payment" on our future inheritance of immortality:

> *For in this we groan, earnestly desiring to be clothed upon with our house which is from heaven. . . . For we that are in this tabernacle do groan, being burdened: not for that we would be unclothed, but clothed upon, that mortality might be swallowed up by life. Now He Who hath wrought us for the selfsame thing is God, Who also hath given unto us the earnest of the Spirit* (2 Corinthians 5:2-5).

We await the coming of the kingdom of God, and yet, our Lord said, *The kingdom of God is within you* (Luke 17:21). The Holy Spirit makes present the kingdom of God as He dwells within those who have been anointed. Through the Spirit we partake, here and now, of the kingdom that is to come.

With such great grace, however, comes great responsibility: *unto whomsoever much is given, of him shall be much required* (Luke 12:48). Having been anointed with the Spirit of God, we have become temples of His holiness. It behooves us, therefore, to live in accordance with this great honor: *Know ye not that ye are the temple of God, and that the Spirit of God dwelleth in you? If any man defile the temple of God, him shall God destroy; for the temple of God is holy, Whose temple ye are* (1 Corinthians 3:16-17).

CHAPTER THIRTEEN
THE FATHERS SPEAK

And ye were first anointed on your forehead, that ye might be delivered from the shame, which the first man, when he had transgressed, bore about with him everywhere; and that *with open face ye might behold as in a glass the glory of the Lord* (2 Corinthians 3:18). Then on your ears; that ye might receive ears quick to hear the divine mysteries, of which Esaias has said, *The Lord wakened mine ear to hear* (Isaiah 50:4); and the Lord Jesus in the Gospel, *He that hath ears to hear let him hear* (Matthew 11:15). Then on your nostrils; that receiving the sacred Ointment ye may say, *We are to God a sweet savor of Christ, in them that are saved* (2 Corinthians 2:15). Then on your breast; that having put on the breastplate of righteousness, ye may stand against the wiles of the devil (cf. Ephesians 6: 14, 11). For as Christ after His Baptism, and the descent of the Holy Spirit, went forth and vanquished the adversary, so likewise, having, after Holy Baptism and the Mystical Chrism, put on the whole armor of the Holy Spirit, do ye stand against the power of the enemy and vanquish it, saying, *I can do all things through Christ Who strengtheneth me* (Philippians 4:13).

Keep this unspotted. . . . For this holy thing is a spiritual preservative of the body, and a safeguard of the soul. . . . Having been anointed, therefore, with this Holy Ointment, keep it unspotted and unblemished in you, pressing forward by good works, and becoming well-pleasing to the Captain of your salvation, Christ Jesus, to Whom be glory for ever and ever. Amen.

St. Cyril of Jerusalem
from the *Lectures on the Christian Sacraments*
SVS Press, 1986

THE SEAL OF THE GIFT OF THE HOLY SPIRIT

Special Study
The Fruit of the Spirit

The Apostle Paul contrasts life lived according to the flesh with that lived according to the Spirit of God. By "flesh" he does not mean the body, but, rather, man's sinful inclinations, that is to say, our old nature. While Baptism is our death and resurrection in Christ, we must nevertheless struggle against our sinful passions, constantly warring against the attacks of our enemy: *For we wrestle not against flesh and blood, but against principalities, against powers, against the rulers of the darkness of this world, against spiritual wickedness in high places* (Ephesians 6:12).

The Apostle tells us that among the works of the flesh are *adultery, fornication, uncleanness, lasciviousness, idolatry, witchcraft, hatred, strife, jealousy, wrath, selfishness, dissensions, heresies, envyings, murders, drunkenness, carousings, and such like* (Galatians 5:19-21). It is shameful for those who are co-heirs with Christ and anointed with the Holy Spirit to do such things.

We are called to live a life consonant with the Spirit, Whom we have received. Those who live according to the Spirit of God need no external set of laws and regulations to guide them, for the Spirit Himself teaches them. When we walk according to the Spirit, then we begin to bear the fruit proper to godly living: *But the*

CHAPTER THIRTEEN

fruit of the Spirit is love, joy, peace, longsuffering, gentleness, goodness, faith, meekness, temperance: against such there is no law (Galatians 5:22-23).

St. Makarios of Egypt taught that all of our spiritual efforts were useless unless we acquire the fruit of the Spirit, for these are the testimony that we are truly living life in accordance with the will of God:

> When we cultivate a vineyard, the whole of our attention and labor is given in the expectation of the vintages.... Similarly, if through the activity of the Spirit we do not perceive within ourselves the fruits of love, peace, joy and the other qualities mentioned by St. Paul, and cannot affirm this with all assurance and spiritual awareness, then our labor for the sake of virginity, prayer, psalmody, fasting and vigil is useless (*The Philokalia*, vol. 3).

Let us examine the first three of these fruits. The first fruit of the Spirit is love. Concerning this St. Maximus the Confessor wrote:

> The one who loves God cannot help but love also every man as himself, even though he is displeased by the passions of those who are not yet purified. ... The one who sees a trace of hatred in his own heart through any fault at all toward any man, whoever he may be, makes himself completely foreign to the love for God, because love for God in no way admits of hatred for man (*The Four Hundred Chapters on Love*).

The second fruit of the Spirit is joy. St. Peter of Damaskos explained the source of this fruit:

THE SEAL OF THE GIFT OF THE HOLY SPIRIT

Nature teaches us rather to grieve, since life is full of pain and effort, like a state of exile dominated by sin. But if a person is constantly mindful of God, he will rejoice: as the Psalmist says, *I remembered God, and I rejoiced* (*The Philokalia*, vol. 3).

St. Peter of Damaskos also explained the nature of true peace—the third fruit of the Spirit—and how it is related to our battle with the passions:

> In a similar way, each of us faithful is attacked and led astray by the passions; but if he is at peace with God and with his neighbor, he overcomes them all. These passions are the 'world' that St. John the Theologian told us to hate, meaning that we are to hate, not God's creatures, but worldly desires. The soul is at peace with God when it is at peace with itself and has become wholly deiform. It is also at peace with God when it is at peace with all men, even if it suffers terrible things at their hands (*The Philokalia*, vol. 3).

On the Day of Judgment, each of us shall be judged according to the fruit that our life bears. What harvest shall we present before the Lord our Judge?

> *A good tree cannot bring forth evil fruit, neither can a corrupt tree bring forth good fruit. Every tree that bringeth not forth good fruit is hewn down, and cast into the fire. Wherefore by their fruits ye shall know them. Not every one that saith unto me, "Lord, Lord," shall enter into the kingdom of heaven; but he that doeth the will of My Father Who is in heaven* (Matthew 7:18-21).

CHAPTER THIRTEEN

Reflection

1. What happened to Christ immediately following His Baptism in the Jordan River?

2. To whom does the authority to confer the Spirit belong?

3. From where does the parish priest get the Holy Chrism?

4. What is the role of the Holy Spirit in our relationship with Christ and the Father?

5. What is the meaning of the Aramaic word, *Abba*?

6. How is the Mystery of Baptism and Chrismation similar to the consecration of Old Testament priests?

7. Is it true that the ordained clergy are the only ministers in the Church?

8. How do the gifts of the Spirit relate to the unity of the Church?

9. In what way is Holy Chrism a "down payment" on our future inheritance?

10. Name five of the fruits of the Spirit listed by St. Paul.

Chapter Fourteen
The Mystical Supper

In the Holy Eucharist we offer to God the substance of our life and receive it back as the Body and Blood of Christ for the sanctification of our souls and bodies and as the mystery of the Church's unity in Christ.

St. Paul once addressed the philosophers of Athens, introducing them to the one true God. During his sermon on Mars' Hill, quoting one of the Greek poets, he said of God, *"in Him we live, and move, and have our being"*(Acts 17:28). St. Nicholas Cabasilas interpreted this in terms of the Mysteries of Baptism, Chrismation, and the Eucharist:

> Baptism confers being and in short, existence according to Christ. . . . The anointing with Chrism perfects him who has received birth by infusing into him the energy that befits such a life. The Holy Eucharist preserves and continues this life and health, since the Bread of Life enables us to preserve that which has been acquired and to continue in life. . . . In this way we live in God. We remove our life from this visible world to that world which is not seen by exchanging, not the place, but the very life itself and its mode (*The Life in Christ*).

CHAPTER FOURTEEN

This is, perhaps, the most succinct exposition of the mysteries ever written. The mysteries are not merely "sacred rites"; they are nothing less than our participation in the life of the Holy Trinity. Having been united with Christ in Baptism and empowered by the Holy Spirit, we are led to the Holy Table and partake of the Bread of heaven.

The Holy Eucharist begins with the offering of bread and wine, which the People of God bring to the Church. Bread and wine are the substance of our life—that by which we live in this world. It is important to note that we do not bring grain and grapes, but the fruits of the earth that have been harvested and made by human intellect and effort into bread and wine.

God gave the world to Adam and Eve as a means of communion with Himself. However, they refused this gift and instead made the world into an end in and of itself. By offering the substance of our life to God in love and thanksgiving, we recover the original eucharistic vocation of the human race.

This offering is possible, however, only because Christ—God made flesh—offered Himself upon the Cross for the life of the world. There is one and only one sacrifice. The Eucharist is nothing else than that one sacrifice on the Cross.

The night He was betrayed, Christ ate His Last Supper with His Disciples. He broke the bread and blessed the wine, instructing the Apostles, *"This do in remembrance of Me"* (1 Corinthians 11:24-25). The Eucharist is, therefore, an act of remembrance; it orients our life toward the Cross.

THE MYSTICAL SUPPER

The New Testament word for remembrance, however, means more than mere psychological recollection. *Anamnesis* literally means to re-present or make present. In the Holy Eucharist we do not remember the sacrifice of Christ on the Cross in the same way we recollect a past event in our own lives; rather, that sacrifice is made present to us. We *participate* in that sacrifice.

There is no doubt that the early Christians understood the Eucharist as a sacrifice. In the first-century Syrian church manual called the *Didache* we read,

> On the Lord's Day assemble together and break bread and give thanks, first making public confession of your faults, that your sacrifice may be pure. . . . For this is the sacrifice spoken of by the Lord: *In every place and time offer me a pure sacrifice. . .* (Malachi 1:11, 14)

We do not offer a *new* sacrifice, however, but the sacrifice that Christ offered once and for all: "For it is Thou, O Christ our God, Who offereth and art offered" (Litur-gy of St. John Chrysostom).

God the Father receives this offering at our hands precisely because it is the offering of His Son. From all eternity the Son receives His being from the Father and, in return, offers Himself to His Father in love. On the Cross, Christ offered Himself to His Father *as man*, thereby introducing humanity into this dynamic movement of Trinitarian love. In the Eucharist our life is offered to the Father in and through Christ, and we receive *eternal* life in return by partaking of the life-giving Body and Blood of the Lord.

CHAPTER FOURTEEN

Verily, verily, I say unto you, Except ye eat the Flesh of the Son of Man, and drink His Blood, ye have no life in you (John 6:53). When Christ spoke these words, many ceased to follow Him (John 6:66). Those who remained, however, became partakers of His Body and Blood: *Take, eat: this is My Body. . . . This is My Blood of the New Testament, which is shed for many for the remission of sins* (Mark 26:26, 28).

In the early years of the Christian era, a problem arose in the Corinthian Church concerning the Eucharist. Many treated it shamefully, using it as an excuse for selfishness and division, rather than as a sacrifice of love and unity. St. Paul warned them of the consequences of their actions:

> *Wherefore whosoever shall eat this Bread, and drink this Cup of the Lord, unworthily, shall be guilty of the Body and Blood of the Lord. But let a man examine himself, and so let him eat of that Bread, and drink of that Cup. For he that eateth and drinketh unworthily, eateth and drinketh damnation to himself, not discerning the Lord's Body. For this cause many are weak and sickly among you, and many sleep* (1 Corinthians 11:27-30).

Thus, according to St. Paul, many have physically died from partaking of the Lord's Table unworthily.

The reason for this is clear, as St. Paul explained: *The Cup of Blessing which we bless, is it not the communion of the Blood of Christ? The Bread which we break, is it not the communion of the Body of Christ* (1 Corinthians 10:16)? In partaking of the Eucharist, we are literally partaking of the Body and Blood of our Lord Jesus Christ.

THE MYSTICAL SUPPER

Early in the second century, St. Ignatius wrote of a sect in the Church that did not believe that Christ had come in the flesh. He noted that they did not attend the eucharistic gathering of the Church. Why? "They abstain from Eucharist and prayer, because they do not confess that the Eucharist is the Flesh of our Savior Jesus Christ" (*Epistle to the Smyrnaeans*). To deny the reality of Christ's humanity is to deny the reality of His presence in the Eucharist and vice versa.

Around the year A.D. 150, St. Justin the Philosopher wrote to the Roman Emperor, explaining to him the Gospel of Christ and petitioning for an end to persecution. Concerning the Eucharist he wrote:

> We do not receive these Gifts as ordinary food or ordinary drink. But as Jesus Christ our Savior was made flesh through the Word of God, and took flesh and blood for our salvation; in the same way the food over which thanksgiving has been offered through the prayer of the Word which we have from Him — the food by which our blood and flesh are nourished through its transformation — is, we are taught, the Flesh and Blood of Jesus Who was made flesh (*Apology* I).

The Mystery of the Eucharist is, therefore, truly awesome. By it we receive into our soul and body the Body and Blood of Christ Himself, Who infuses His divine life into our life. All of this is accomplished through our sacramental participation in His Cross.

Something else happens during the mystery, however. We remember not only the sacrifice of the Cross, which took place once and for all almost two thousand

CHAPTER FOURTEEN

years ago; we also remember the future. In the Liturgy, between the words of institution ("This is My Body...") and the *epiclesis* (the invocation of the Holy Spirit), the priest prays:

> Remembering this saving commandment and all that has come to pass for us, the Cross, the tomb, the Resurrection on the third day, the Ascension into heaven, the sitting at the right hand, and *the Second and Glorious Coming...*"

Thus, in the Liturgy, we remember the Second Coming of Christ, which, obviously, has yet to happen. We have said that the Holy Spirit is the pledge of the kingdom to come. It is the action of the Spirit that makes the sacrifice of Christ present to us, that transforms the bread and wine into the Body and Blood of Christ, and that makes present the future kingdom.

At the Last Supper our Lord told the Apostles, *"But I say unto you, I will not drink henceforth of this fruit of the vine, until that day when I drink it new with you in My Father's kingdom"* (Matthew 26:29). St. Paul adds, *For as often as ye eat this Bread, and drink this Cup, ye do show the Lord's death till He come* (1 Corinthians 11:26). It is clear that from the very beginning, the Eucharist was oriented toward *both* the Cross and the coming kingdom.

The fact that the Eucharist is our sacramental participation in the great Wedding Feast of the kingdom (Matthew 22:2 ff.), underscores one other aspect of the mystery. The Eucharist is given not only for our personal sanctification but also as the sacrament of the Church's unity.

THE MYSTICAL SUPPER

St. Paul writes, *For we being many are one Bread, and one Body: for we are all partakers of that one Bread* (1 Corinthians 10:17). In the early Church, *all* Christians in a given area met together to celebrate the Eucharist at the same place and the same time. In this gathering, social, racial, and political barriers were overcome as all participated in one Liturgy, offering one prayer and partaking of one Bread.

This principle is expressed in canon law today by the fact that a priest may celebrate only one Liturgy during a day. If circumstances necessitate that a second Liturgy be celebrated in a Church, it must be celebrated by a different priest and on a different altar. This may seem to be a somewhat "round-about" approach, but it serves to underscore the principle that the community partakes of *one* Eucharist.

Every Sunday and great feastday the Church in a given location gathers together to celebrate the Eucharist—to offer and be offered to God in love and to receive from Him the "Medicine of Immortality." In so doing, we are united as one Body; we are given the Body and Blood of Christ as our spiritual nourishment, and our whole life is oriented toward both the Cross and the kingdom that is to come.

CHAPTER FOURTEEN

THE FATHERS SPEAK

Give thanks in this manner. First, over the Cup: "We give thanks to Thee, our Father, for the Holy Vine of Thy son David, which Thou hast made known to us through Jesus Thy Son: Thine be the glory forever." Then over the broken Bread: "We give thanks to Thee, our Father, for the life and knowledge which Thou didst make known to us through Jesus Thy Son: Thine be the glory for ever. As this broken Bread was scattered upon the mountains and was gathered together and became one, so let Thy Church be gathered together from the ends of the earth into Thy kingdom: for Thine is the glory and the power through Jesus Christ for ever and ever." Let none eat or drink of this Eucharist of yours except those who have been baptized into the name of the Lord. For on this point the Lord said, *"Do not give what is holy to the dogs"* (Matthew 7:6).

> from the *Didache*
> *The Early Christian Fathers*

It was necessary that the remedy for my weakness be God and become man, for were He God only He would not be united to us, for how could He become our feast? On the other hand, if Christ were no more than what we are, His feast would have been ineffectual. . . . By His divinity He is able to exalt and transcend our human nature and to transform it into Himself. . . . It is clear, then, that Christ infuses Himself into us and mingles Himself with us.

> **St. Nicholas Cabasilas**
> from *The Life in Christ*

THE MYSTICAL SUPPER
Special Study
The Communion of Saints

During the Divine Liturgy, as the Holy Gifts are brought to the altar for consecration, we sing, "Let us who mystically represent the Cherubim and who sing the thrice-holy hymn to the Life-creating Trinity now lay aside all earthly cares." The worship of the Church takes place both on earth and in heaven. Regardless of the physical circumstances in which the Liturgy is celebrated — be it in a great cathedral or in someone's living room — the true locus of the Church's worship is heaven itself.

St. Paul tells us in the Epistle to the Hebrews that the earthly tabernacle of the Old Testament was patterned after the tabernacle in heaven (Hebrews 9:23). It is before the heavenly altar where the worship of the Church takes place, officiated by Christ Himself, our High Priest: *For Christ is not entered into the holy places made with hands, which are the figures of the true; but into heaven itself, now to appear in the presence of God for us* (Hebrews 9:24).

Because the Liturgy of the Church takes place in heaven, it is celebrated in the presence of all the angels and Saints. Traditional Orthodox temples are filled with icons of the Saints, often being covered from floor to ceiling. These icons sacramentally manifest to us the lit-

CHAPTER FOURTEEN

eral presence of the Saints. That is why, upon entering a temple, we venerate the icons. We are greeting the members of our heavenly family as we would greet the members of our earthly family upon entering a room.

The Liturgy is, therefore, a family affair, encompassing both those in heaven and those on earth. Not only is it attended by the whole Church, but it is offered on behalf of the whole Church—indeed, on behalf of the whole world. "Thine own of Thine own, we offer unto Thee, on behalf of all and for all."

Immediately following the consecration of the Holy Gifts, the celebrant begins the great prayer of intercession. Here, the whole Church and all of mankind is gathered together in Christ's intercession before the Father, *seeing He ever liveth to make intercession for them* (Hebrews 7:25):

> Again we offer unto Thee this reasonable worship for those who have fallen asleep in the faith . . . for the whole world; for the holy, catholic, and apostolic Church.

The prayer of Christ the High Priest—therefore the prayer of the Church—is for all mankind, both the living and the dead, for *He is not the God of the dead, but the God of the living* (Mark 12:27). No one falls outside the embrace of the Church's love and intercession.

The offering of prayer and sacrifice for the dead is first recorded in the Scripture in the Second Book of Maccabees. After a battle Judas Maccabeus discovered that his slain men had been wearing tokens of idols. Seeing this, he began to pray for the souls of his men and took up a collection that a sin offering might be made for them in Jerusalem. The reason for this action was their belief in the resurrection of the dead:

> *In doing this he acted very well and honorably, taking account of the resurrection. For if he were not expecting that those who had fallen would rise again, it would have been superfluous and foolish to pray for the dead. But if he was looking to the splendid reward that is laid up for those who fall asleep in godliness, it was a holy and pious thought. Therefore he made atonement for the dead, that they might be delivered from their sin* (2 Maccabees 12:43-45, Revised Standard Version).

As with the doctrine of the Trinity, the doctrine of the resurrection was revealed only gradually. For most of the period of the Old Testament, immortality was thought of in terms of one's progeny. This is why the Law of Moses made no specific provisions for prayer for the dead. By the time of the Maccabees, however, belief in the resurrection had taken root. It remained somewhat controversial, however, well into the period of the New Testament, for there we read of the Sadducees, who denied the resurrection.

With the resurrection of our Lord Jesus Christ, the once-impenetrable barrier of death is removed; death no longer separates us from those we love. The Eucharist is the mystery of our unity in Christ—the unity of those in heaven and those on earth. In the Eucharist, therefore, we experience communion with God and through Him communion with the Saints.

CHAPTER FOURTEEN
Reflection

1. In what ways are the mysteries related to the fact that we *live, and move, and have our being* in God?

2. What do we offer to God in the Eucharist?

3. Whose sacrifice is being offered in the Eucharist?

4. What does the word *anamnesis* mean?

5. How is Christ's sacrifice of Himself as man related to His eternal relationship with the Father?

6. St. Paul says that the Cup of Blessing and the Bread that we bless is communion with what?

7. According to St. Ignatius, why did those who denied that the Lord came in the flesh refuse to attend the Eucharist?

8. How is it that in the Eucharist we remember the future?

9. How does the Eucharist manifest the unity of the Church?

10. Why does the Church pray and offer the Eucharist for the dead?

Chapter Fifteen
The Church at Prayer

Prayer is the language of the Church, with which we communicate with God both privately and corporately.

In the Acts of the Apostles we read that the first Christians *continued steadfastly in the Apostles' doctrine and fellowship, and in the breaking of the Bread, and in the prayers* (Acts 2:42). From the beginning, prayer—both corporate and private—was essential to the life of the Church. Every Orthodox Christian, therefore, is expected to participate fully in the Church's liturgical prayer *and* to have a personal rule of prayer of his or her own.

And the LORD spake unto Moses face to face, as a man speaketh unto his friend (Exodus 33:11). It is through prayer that we communicate with God. We praise Him for His great lovingkindness and entreat His mercy for our sins. We bring before Him our troubles and concerns. We also pray for one another, as St. James enjoins us (James 5:16).

Prayer is, therefore, an expression of the very nature of the Church, which is love. In prayer we not only spend time with our Beloved, we share our love for God with others as we make intercession for their needs. Prayer is the very language of the Church, the "abc's" of our life in Christ.

It is significant that St. Luke mentions *the* prayers. The Jews of Jesus' time prayed specific prayers at specific times of the day. Furthermore, they observed a cycle of fasts and feasts, through which they sanctified their life in this world. The Apostles also observed these practices (cf. Acts 20:16), as do Orthodox Christians today.

The daily cycle of prayer begins in the evening with the service of Vespers. The Church follows the Jewish practice of reckoning the beginning of the day from the setting of the sun: *and the evening and the morning were the first day* (Genesis 1:5). The cycle continues with Compline, which is served after supper; the Midnight Office, Matins (*Orthros*); and the Canonical Hours: First (6 a.m.), Third (9 a.m.), Sixth (noon), and Ninth (3 p.m.).

Through this cycle of prayer, each day is sanctified, set apart, for God:

> *For from the rising of the sun even unto the going down of the same My name shall be great among the Gentiles; and in every place incense shall be offered unto My name, and a pure sacrifice: for My name shall be great among the heathen, saith the* LORD *of hosts* (Malachi 1:11).

This prophecy is important because it clearly points to the Church. Only in the New Testament era is God's name praised among the Gentiles, and only in the Christian Church is incense and a pure sacrifice offered to God throughout the world.

THE CHURCH AT PRAYER

The sanctification of the day is clearly stressed at the "Prayer of the Hours," which is read at every service except Matins and Vespers. In this prayer we are reminded of God's mercy and ask for His guidance throughout the day:

> Thou Who *at all times and at every hour*, both in heaven and on earth, art worshipped and glorified, O Christ God, longsuffering, plenteous in mercy and compassion; Who lovest the just and showest mercy to those who are hardened in sin; Who callest all to salvation through the promise of good things to come: Do Thou, the same Lord, receive also our supplications *at this present time*, and direct our lives according to Thy commandments. Set aright our minds; cleanse our thoughts; and deliver us from all calamity, wrath, and distress. Compass us round about with Thy holy angels, that, guided and guarded by their host, we may attain unto the unity of the faith, and unto the comprehension of Thine ineffable glory. For blessed art Thou unto ages of ages. Amen.

The Daily Office consists primarily of the chanting of the Psalms. The Psalter was the hymnal of Israel, and it remains the primary hymnal of the Church. Every service has specific Psalms assigned to it. For example, the liturgical day begins with Psalm 103[104], which glorifies God for the wonders of creation. In addition, the Psalter is divided into twenty sections, called *kathismata*. These sections are assigned so that the entire Psalter is read during the week. During Lent, the readings from the Psalter double.

CHAPTER FIFTEEN

One should note here that the Divine Liturgy is not counted among the daily services. The Daily Office is tied to specific times of the day; through it we sanctify time. The Liturgy, however, reaches beyond time into eternity. Although it is *usually* served after the Sixth Hour, it cannot be tied to a specific hour of the day.

The Daily Office is served in its entirety only in monasteries and large cathedrals. The fact that most laymen do not have ready access to these services does not mean, however, that we are exempt from the need to sanctify our day through prayer. The ancient Jews had a daily rule of prayer, and so did the first Christians. The *Didache* (first century) instructed Christians to pray the Lord's Prayer three times a day.

For most Orthodox Christians, the daily rule of prayer consists of prayers in the morning, evening, and at meals. To this may be added prayers in special times of need and prayers in preparation for Confession and Communion.

Christians are never forbidden from praying extemporaneously in private, but we are strongly encouraged to use the prayers of the Church that have been sanctified by their use through the centuries. By using the prayers of the Church, we are assured that our prayers are in accordance with the will of God, thus avoiding the problem mentioned by St. James: *Ye ask, and receive not, because ye ask amiss* (James 4:3).

Every Orthodox Christian should discuss his rule of prayer with his spiritual father. This is both an act of submission of our personal will to the will of the Church and a practical safeguard against doing more or less than we should. All spiritual guides agree that it is better to pray a short rule of prayer with attention and devotion than to try to rush through a long rule. The point is to have a practical rule of prayer and stick to it.

In addition to the daily cycle of prayer, there are also the weekly, yearly, and Paschal cycles that determine the theme of a particular day. The weekly cycle begins with Sunday, on which we commemorate the Resurrection. Each and every Sunday is a miniature Pascha. On Monday we commemorate the holy angels, on Tuesday St. John the Forerunner, on Wednesday and Friday the Cross, on Thursday the Apostles and St. Nicholas, and on Saturday the martyrs and the departed faithful. Because of the commemoration of the Cross, Wednesday and Friday are set apart as fast days.

The yearly cycle refers to those feasts and fasts that occur on fixed dates of the year. Various Saints are commemorated each day of the year, but certain commemorations are given more emphasis than others. There are twelve "Great Feasts" of the Church, nine of which are assigned specific dates.

The Church year begins on September 1. It is significant that the first Great Feast of the year commemorates the Nativity of the Theotokos (September 8), and the last commemorates her Falling Asleep (August 15). We have seen that the Mother of God is both the personification of the Church and the role model for each Christian. There is a real sense, therefore, in which *our* life, from the cradle to the grave, is taken up and celebrated in the yearly liturgical cycle.

CHAPTER FIFTEEN

The hymns proper to the daily commemorations of the yearly cycle are found in a twelve-volume set called the *Menaion*. Every Orthodox Christian should have a copy of *The Festal Menaion*, which contains the hymns for the Great Feasts. These hymns are the prayers of the Church, through which we praise God and are ourselves taught and conformed to His image:

> *Let the word of Christ dwell in you richly in all wisdom; teaching and admonishing one another in psalms and hymns and spiritual songs, singing with grace in your hearts to the Lord* (Colossians 3:16).

The Great and Holy Pascha (Easter) is the "Feast of Feasts." The Paschal cycle, the date of which varies from year to year, begins with Great Lent, includes the Entrance of the Lord into Jerusalem, Holy Week, Pascha itself, the Ascension, and the Feast of Pentecost.

The hymns for Great Lent are included in *The Lenten Triodion*, and those for Pascha make up *The Pentecostarion*. *The Lenten Triodion* is perhaps the single richest literary source of spiritual nourishment the Church has to offer. It includes the Great Canon of St. Andrew of Crete, which is a long meditation on the biblical images of repentance.

There is one other form of prayer that is not related to any of the liturgical cycles. It is the most personal and most misunderstood prayer of the Church: the "Prayer of the Heart" or the "Jesus Prayer." This prayer consists of the constant repetition of a short prayer centered on the name of Jesus. The most common form is: "Lord Jesus Christ, Son of God, have mercy on me, the sinner."

THE CHURCH AT PRAYER

The Fathers understand this prayer as the fulfillment of St. Paul's admonition, *Pray without ceasing* (1 Thessalonians 5:17). The Jesus Prayer, however, is not a mantra. Its importance derives not from its repetition, but from its doctrinal and ethical content and from the fact that we are addressing a person. In the prayer we affirm our belief in the divinity of Christ and confess our own sinfulness. Through this constant invocation of the name of Jesus, the heart is purified and receives divine grace.

Although all Orthodox Christians should say the Jesus Prayer whenever possible, there are certain meditative techniques associated with this prayer that are practiced only by experienced monks and nuns. A layman should simply recite the Jesus Prayer slowly with great attention. Under no circumstances, however, should he attempt to regulate his breathing or try any other "technique" without the personal approval and guidance of a spiritual father experienced in the Jesus Prayer.

When we are in Church, we pray the prayers of the Church. At home we keep a personal rule of prayer, sanctifying each day. In times of great joy or trouble, we cry out to God from the depths of our heart with thanksgiving and entreaty. At other times, such as when performing mundane tasks, we have the Prayer of Jesus to occupy our mind and spirit and direct our attention toward our Lord. In this way, prayer becomes the very substance of our life, the very air that we breathe.

CHAPTER FIFTEEN

THE FATHERS SPEAK

Prayer is by nature a dialog and a union of man with God. Its effect is to hold the world together. It achieves a reconciliation with God.

Pray in all simplicity. The publican and the prodigal son were reconciled to God by a single utterance.

The attitude of prayer is the same for all, but there are many kinds of prayer and many different prayers.

But heartfelt thanksgiving should have first place in our book of prayer. Next should be confession and genuine contrition of soul. After that should come our request to the universal King. This method of prayer is best, as one of the brothers was told by an angel of the Lord.

If you ever find yourself having to appear before a human judge, you may use that as an example of how to conduct yourself in prayer. Perhaps you have never stood before a judge or witnessed a cross-examination. In that case, take your cue from the way patients appeal to surgeons prior to an operation or a cautery.

In your prayers there is no need for high-flown words, for it is the simple and unsophisticated babblings of children that have more often won the heart of the Father in heaven.

St. John Climacus
from *The Ladder of Divine Ascent*
Tr. by Colm Luibheid
Paulist Press, 1982

THE CHURCH AT PRAYER
Special Study
Fasting

In the New Testament, prayer is closely associated with fasting. When the Apostles were unable to cast a demon out of a child, the Lord told them, "*This kind can come forth by nothing, but by prayer and fasting*" (Mark 9:29). Even though He is God by nature, our Lord Himself fasted in the flesh so that that we might learn the importance of fasting (cf. Matthew 4:2).

In giving instructions to His Apostles, Christ did not say to them, "*If* ye fast," but "*When ye fast*" (Matthew 6:16). The Apostles fasted (cf. Acts 13:2). In the *Didache* we read that the early Christians observed Wednesdays and Fridays as regular fast days, even as we do today.

Fasting is, therefore, not an option for Orthodox Christians. It is an essential element of the life in Christ. Great Lent begins with this command from the Prophecy of Joel: *Blow the trumpet in Zion, sanctify a fast, call a solemn assembly* (Joel 2:15). In short, fasting is a matter of obedience to God.

There are two kinds of fasting: (1) a complete abstinence from food and (2) an abstinence from certain kinds of food. Complete abstinence from food is prescribed before the reception of Communion. This begins the evening before Communion. The *minimum* requirement is no food or drink after midnight. Many also ob-

CHAPTER FIFTEEN

serve a complete fast at the beginning of Lent and on Great and Holy Friday, at least until after Vespers.

During Great Lent and the other seasons of fasting, we abstain from all meat, dairy products, and fish with backbones. We also regulate the amount of food eaten. The Fathers tell us that we should get up from the table still slightly hungry, in order to be attentive at prayer.

Abstinence from certain types of food has nothing to do with "uncleanness." There is nothing morally wrong with eating meat, although most Fathers did teach that Adam and Eve did not eat meat before the Fall. There is, however, a correlation between the types of food we eat and our spiritual state. Animal products, especially fats and oils, tend to inflame the passions and create inner turmoil. This ancient wisdom of the Fathers will come as no surprise to modern nutritionists.

Although fasting has many health benefits to recommend it, that is not the reason we fast. Bishop Kallistos writes, "The primary aim of fasting is to make us conscious of our dependence upon God" (*The Lenten Triodion*, p. 16). We voluntarily experience physical hunger in order to make us aware of our true spiritual hunger, our poverty of spirit.

Another reason we fast is to subdue our passions and self-will. The Fathers tell us that there is no way we can control our urges for sexual gratification, money, power, etc., if we are unable to control our stomachs. Fasting is the first step toward self-control.

When we fast, it is extremely important that we do so according to the rules of the Church and the directions of our spiritual father. Self-will is cut off by obedience. Making up our own fasting rules is an act of self-will, not obedience, and can only lead to spiritual pride.

Fasting, therefore, is a means of subduing the passions; it is not a virtue in and of itself. We do not fast in order to earn "merits." We are servants of our heavenly Master and do only as we are commanded:

> *So likewise ye, when ye shall have done all those things which are commanded you, say, "We are unprofitable servants: we have done that which was our duty to do"* (Luke 17:10).

As with any practice, fasting can become an excuse for legalism. It is possible to keep the letter of the fast and yet violate its inner spirit. We must always keep in mind that the purpose of fasting is to control our passions and to bring us closer to God. Strict fasting according the rules that is not accompanied by an inner attitude of submission to God yields only a hypocritical and judgmental attitude toward others. This is why we are enjoined by the hymns of the Church to observe a spiritual as well as a physical fast:

> Let us set out with joy upon the season of the Fast, and prepare ourselves for spiritual combat. Let us purify our soul and cleanse our flesh; and as we fast from food, let us abstain also from every passion. Rejoicing in the virtues of the Spirit may we persevere with love (*The Lenten Triodion*).

CHAPTER FIFTEEN

Reflection

1. How were the spiritual practices of the Apostles related to the practices of the Jews of that time?

2. When does the liturgical day begin?

3. What is the first service of the day?

4. What is the primary hymnal of the Church?

5. What is a *kathisma*?

6. Why do we need a personal rule of prayer?

7. When does the Church year begin?

8. What is the "Feast of Feasts"?

9. Can laypeople use the Jesus Prayer?

10. What is the purpose of fasting?

Chapter Sixteen
The Mystery of Love

Holy Matrimony is a mystery of the Church in which the man and wife work out their salvation in love and submission, serving as a living icon of Christ's relationship with the Church.

Our Lord's first public miracle was at a wedding in Cana of Galilee (cf. John 2:1 ff.). According to the Fathers, Christ is present at every Christian wedding, blessing the couple's new life together. Christian marriage is not simply a legal contract; it is a relationship in which the partners work out their salvation together. It is also a living icon of Christ's relationship with the Church.

Immediately after the account of the creation of man, the Book of Genesis records: *And the LORD God said, "It is not good that the man should be alone; I will make him an help meet for him"* (Genesis 2:18). He took Eve from the side of Adam, and Adam said: *"This is now bone of my bones, and flesh of my flesh: she shall be called woman, because she was taken out of man"* (Genesis 2:23).

God gave the couple the commandment to go forth and multiply and people the earth (Genesis 1:28). In the beginning, procreation was the primary purpose of marriage. We have seen that initially Israel had no clear concept of life after death. Immortality consisted in leaving behind progeny. This is why the inability to bear children was considered such a curse, and why a man was allowed to have children by a concubine (cf. Genesis 16:1-4).

With the coming of Christ, however, mankind's understanding of life and eternal life changed radically. Our Lord entered into the realm of death—*sheol* or *hades*—in order to abolish its power. No longer held captive, mankind arose with Christ to participate in the unending life of the Holy Trinity.

With the Resurrection of Christ came a renewed understanding of the nature of marriage. Personal immortality through the resurrection eliminated the necessity of procreation as a means of survival. This is why our Lord told the Sadducees, *For in the resurrection they neither marry, nor are given in marriage, but are as the angels of God in heaven* (Matthew 22:30).

In Christ the true nature of marriage is revealed; marriage is an end in and of itself. To understand this, however, we must first understand the nature and purpose of man's sexual drive.

We have said that man's nature possesses certain faculties or energies. One of these is the erotic power, the power of sexual desire. In the animal kingdom this desire guarantees the survival of the species. In human beings, however, this desire is related directly to the realization of the image of God within us. Archimandrite George writes:

> But what—more than anything else—manifests the imprint of God on the human soul is the power of

THE MYSTERY OF LOVE

desire (eros) within the soul . . . and the impetus which a sanctified eros lends the soul in its movement towards its divine archetype. The Saints, especially Maximus the Confessor and Dionysius the Areopagite, understand this power of eroticism as not referring simply to human sexual desire. To put it better, the sexual urge is an expression of that natural yearning which is implanted within us by our Creator, and leads us toward Him (*The Eros of Repentance*, pp. 2-3).

Thus, according to the Holy Fathers, our sexual desire is but a manifestation of the deeper desire of the soul for union with God. The Song of Songs is an erotic poem that was accepted into the canon of the Hebrew and Christian Scriptures precisely because human eros is fundamentally a thirst for the divine. The human soul longs to say of her God: *My Beloved is mine, and I am His.* (Song of Songs 2:16).

When man fell, his natural energies became corrupted. We do not experience sexuality as God created it, but as a passion that rules our life. We are so used to this situation that we have come to consider our deviancies as normal.

Sexual passion is one of the primary expressions of fallen man's egoism. Sex becomes a tool by which we gain dominance over others. Through the eyes of lust, others cease to be personal *subjects*—bearers of the divine image—and become *objects* of our inordinate desires. We perceive ourselves, individually, to be the center of the universe. All others exist in order to fulfill our desires.

CHAPTER SIXTEEN

It is significant that before the Fall Adam and Eve had no knowledge of their nakedness: *And they were both naked, the man and his wife, and were not ashamed* (Genesis 2:25). It was not until their transgression that they realized they had no clothes. What happened? They ceased to look upon one another with that purity of vision with which they were originally created. The other became an object of lust.

Our sexual drive was given to us by God and is good by nature; it is the misuse of that desire that is sinful. There are two ways whereby our erotic energies are sanctified and returned to their proper state: celibacy and marriage. We shall discuss celibacy in regard to monasticism in the next chapter. For now let us focus our attention on the sanctifying power of marriage.

The first purpose of Christian marriage is to focus our sexual energies on *one person* as long as we live. We should not think of marriage as the "legalization" of a desire that is otherwise sinful. Rather, we must understand the positive, transformative power of marriage.

It is often said that man is not naturally monogamous. This, of course, is a misuse of the term *natural*. What we often consider "natural" is the state of fallen or sub-nature. Indeed, it is difficult for fallen man to be monogamous. Through the Mystery of Holy Matrimony, however, divine grace is given to the couple that their marriage bed be undefiled.

It is significant that unfaithfulness is the one condition that Jesus allowed for divorce:

> *They say unto Him, "Why did Moses then command to give a writing of divorce, and to put her away?" He saith*

> unto them, "Moses because of the hardness of your hearts suffered you to put away your wives: but from the beginning it was not so. And I say unto you, Whosoever shall put away his wife, except it be for fornication, and shall marry another, committeth adultery: and whoso marrieth her which is put away doth commit adultery" (Matthew 19:7-9).

Defilement of the marriage bed destroys the bond of love, and, hence, the marriage.

The second purpose of marriage is the subjugation of the partners' egos. There is a definite order within the marriage relationship that serves as an icon of God's relationship to the world and of Christ's relationship to the Church:

> For this cause shall a man leave his father and mother, and shall be joined unto his wife, and they two shall be one flesh. This is a great mystery: but I speak concerning Christ and the Church. (Ephesians 5:31-32).

The mutual submission of the marriage partners is directly tied to this iconic relationship.

God could have created human beings as a single sex with an asexual reproductive system. However, He chose to make human nature disexual: *So God created man in His own image, in the image of God created He him; male and female created He them* (Genesis 1:27). The difference between the male and female reflects the difference between the uncreated God and the created world.

The male images forth God and the female the world. This iconic relationship is expressed in marriage in the proper relationship between husband and wife.

CHAPTER SIXTEEN

The husband is the head of the household. The family should relate to the husband and father as to the Lord:

> *Wives, submit yourselves unto your own husbands, as unto the Lord. For the husband is the head of the wife, even as Christ is the head of the Church: and He is the Savior of the body. Therefore as the Church is subject unto Christ, so let the wives be to their own husbands in every thing* (Ephesians 5:22-23).

Headship, however, is a position of responsibility, not privilege. The husband is to give his life for his wife and family as Christ gave His life for the Church:

> *Husbands, love your wives, even as Christ also loved the Church, and gave Himself for Her; that He might sanctify and cleanse Her with the washing of water by the Word, that He might present Her to Himself a glorious Church, not having spot, or wrinkle, or any such thing; but that She should be holy and without blemish. So ought men to love their wives as their own bodies. He that loveth his wife loveth himself. For no man ever yet hated his own flesh; but nourisheth and cherisheth it, even as the Lord the Church* (Ephesians 5:25-28):

The wife subjugates her will to the husband, and the husband subjugates his will to the good of the family. In this way the egoism of both partners is overcome. Both learn to live in and with and for the other, experiencing in this life a foretaste of the eternal Trinitarian communion.

It should be noted that where sexual relations are concerned, both partners are to submit to one another. The wife has exactly the same claims upon her husband as he has upon her:

THE MYSTERY OF LOVE

The wife hath not power of her own body, but the husband: and likewise also the husband hath not power of his own body, but the wife. Defraud ye not one the other, except it be with consent for a time, that ye may give yourselves to fasting and prayer; and come together again, that Satan tempt you not for your incontinence (1 Corinthians 7:4-5).

Through the Mystery of Marriage, therefore, man's sexual energies are properly channeled, and his ego is overcome through mutual submission. In doing so, the couple serves as an icon of Christ's union with His Bride, the Church, participating in that union.

The natural fruit of this sanctified, erotic communion is the begetting of children, for love is productive by nature. The Church does not define reproduction as the *purpose* of marriage, but its natural consequence.

It is only natural that a couple would wish to share their love with the fruit of that love. In this way the love of the two reaches beyond itself and becomes *shared* love. The family then images forth not only the union of God with man, but also the union of love shared between the persons of the All-holy Trinity.

CHAPTER SIXTEEN
THE FATHERS SPEAK

You have seen the amount of obedience necessary; now hear about the amount of love necessary. Do you want your wife to be obedient to you, as the Church is to Christ? Then be responsible for the same providential care of her, as Christ is for the Church. And even if it becomes necessary for you to give your life for her, yes, and even to endure and undergo suffering of any kind, do not refuse. . . . In the same way, then, as He honored Her by putting at His feet one who turned Her back on Him . . . as He accomplished this not with threats, or violence, or terror, or anything else like that, but through His untiring love; so also you should behave toward your wife. Even if you see her belittling you, or despising and mocking you, still you will be able to subject her to yourself, through affection, kindness, and your great regard for her. There is no influence more powerful than the bond of love, especially for husband and wife. A servant can be taught submission through fear; but even he, if provoked too much, will soon seek his escape. But one's partner for life, the mother of one's children, the source of one's every joy, should never be fettered with fear and threats, but with love and patience. What kind of marriage can there be when the wife is afraid of her husband? What sort of satisfaction could a husband himself have, if he lives with his wife as if she were a slave, and not with a woman by her own free will? Suffer anything for her sake, but never disgrace her, for Christ never did this with the Church.

St. John Chrysostom
from *On Marriage and Family Life*
Tr. by C. Roth and D. Anderson
SVS Press, 1986

THE MYSTERY OF LOVE
Special Study
God and Gender

Few issues are as explosive in our society as those involving gender and religion. The Orthodox Christian addresses these issues within the framework of the Church's self-understanding as the Bride of Christ. Whether the issue at hand is "inclusive language," the role of women in the Church, or homosexual desire, the answer lies in the great mystery: Christ and the Church.

The peoples of the ancient world frequently worshipped female deities, accepted priestesses, and thought nothing of homosexual behavior. Israel, however, stood alone in rejecting all of these practices. The reason for this lies in God's revelation of Himself as being radically distinct from His creation.

We have said that the world was created *ex nihilo*. Between the being of God and the being of the world there is an irreducible gulf. The world is not God, has never been God, and will never be God. The fact that God has united creation to Himself in the Incarnation in no way destroys the distinction between the Uncreated and the created. In Christ we participate in the uncreated grace of God, becoming by that grace what He is by nature, yet we never cease being creatures; our created nature is *never* transformed into the divine nature.

This difference between God and the world is expressed iconically by the disexuality of human nature. In the Divine Scriptures, God is *always* represented by

CHAPTER SIXTEEN

the male and creation by the female. God is the Bridegroom, and the world — or more precisely, the Church, which is the world recreated in Christ — is the Bride.

God, of course, is neither male nor female; He is beyond all such created concepts. Nevertheless, He has given us certain images and concepts whereby we have come to know Him. Though these concepts can never fully describe or define the indescribable God, we are nonetheless bound by them.

It is true that the Scriptures occasionally use female imagery in regard to God. For example, Christ said of Jerusalem: *O Jerusalem, Jerusalem . . . how often would I have gathered thy children together, even as a hen gathereth her chickens under her wings, and ye would not* (Matthew 23:37). This is, however, a simile. Christ called God "Father," not "Mother." Christ is the "Son" of God, not the "Daughter" of God.

The use of "inclusive" or even gender-neutral language about God is an egregious violation of the integrity of the Scriptures and of the Liturgy. To call God "Mother" is nothing less than to introduce a *different* god. Inclusive language blurs the distinction between the Creator and creation, elevating the creation (that is, the female) to the place of God, and thereby returning us once again to the Original Sin.

From this it should be evident why it is impossible for the Church to have priestesses. The male, because he is a creature, can represent God only iconically. The female, however, *is* creation. The Church is essentially *female*. If, therefore, the priest — who is the image of Christ the Bridegroom — is a female, then what happens to the male principle? Once again, the distinction between Creator and creation is destroyed, and a new religion is born. Actually, it is an *old* religion that is reborn—the religion of pantheism, which Israel and the Church rejected.

The inherent disexuality of human nature and its iconic relationship to Christ and the Church also explains the Church's attitude toward homosexual desire. Notice the context in which St. Paul addresses this issue:

> *Who changed the truth of God into the lie, and worshipped and served the creature more than the Creator, Who is blessed for ever. For this cause God gave them up unto vile affections: for even their women did change the natural use into that which is against nature: And likewise also the men, leaving the natural use of the woman, burned in their lust one toward another; men with men working that which is unseemly, and receiving in themselves that recompense of their error which was meet* (Romans 1:25-27).

For St. Paul, homosexual desire is not only a result of the Fall, it is actually paradigmatic of the Fall, much in the same way that marriage is paradigmatic of Christ's saving relationship to the Church. It is clear, therefore, that the Church cannot bless homosexual activity. Human sexuality can be rightly expressed only in Holy Matrimony or in celibacy.

CHAPTER SIXTEEN

Reflection

1. Where did our Lord perform His first public miracle?

2. How does the Resurrection of Christ affect our understanding of the purpose of marriage?

3. How did the Fathers understand the power of human eroticism?

4. Why did Adam and Even not realize they were naked before the Fall?

5. What is the first reason for marriage?

6. W hat is the only reason Jesus allowed for divorce?

7. Whom does the husband image forth in marriage? Whom does the wife image forth?

8. What is the responsibility of the wife in marriage?

9. What is the responsibility of the husband?

10. What role do children play in marriage?

Chapter Seventeen
Monasticism

Monks and nuns are the scientists of the spiritual world, using prayer, renunciation, fasting, and obedience as their tools in exploring the depths of the human soul.

The family is a Church in miniature. Within its circle of love the husband, wife, and children work out their salvation together. While the vast majority of Christians are called to live out their lives in Holy Matrimony, some are called to walk a different path.

St. Paul explains that the responsibilities of marriage and the cares of life in the world can distract our attention away from our relationship with Christ:

> *But I would have you without carefulness. He that is unmarried careth for the things that belong to the Lord, how he may please the Lord. But he that is married careth for the things that are of the world, how he may please his wife. There is difference also between a wife and a virgin. The unmarried woman careth for the things of the Lord, that she may be holy both in body and in spirit: but she that is married careth for the things of the world, how she may please her husband* (1 Corinthians 7:32-34).

MONASTICISM

St. Paul is not saying that marriage is bad. Indeed, the Church excommunicates those who say that it is evil (Council of Gangra). It is obvious, however, that married life entails responsibilities that the celibate life does not. This is why St. Paul writes: *For I would that all men were even as I myself* (that is, unmarried). *But every man hath his proper gift of God, one after this manner, and another after that* (1 Corinthians 7:7).

Notice that St. Paul speaks of the celibate life as a gift of God. It is not a life that we are able to live on our own power. Our Lord taught the same thing. After He explained to His Disciples that a man is to have only one wife for his lifetime, the Disciples replied:

> *"If the case of the man be so with his wife, it is not good to marry." But He said unto them, "All men cannot receive this saying, save they to whom it is given. For there are some eunuchs, which were so born from their mother's womb: and there are some eunuchs, which were made eunuchs of men: and there be eunuchs, which have made themselves eunuchs for the kingdom of heaven's sake. He that is able to receive it, let him receive it"* (Mat 19:10-12).

The celibate life, therefore, is for those who are able to receive it.

Celibates living in the world, however, must deal with many of the same temptations and distractions as married couples. For this reason the Church offers the possibility of consecrating oneself *solely* to the task of one's salvation. Monasticism is the consecration of the celibate life. It is a life devoted exclusively to repentance, prayer, and service to God.

CHAPTER SEVENTEEN

Monasticism as we know it today developed in the fourth century, but the idea of consecrating one's life solely to the work of God is much older. The prophets of the Old Testament, particularly St. John the Baptist[†], are the prototypical monks. In the early Church, widows and virgins constituted a distinct order within the community. To be accepted to the order of widows, a woman had to be of a certain age and spiritual maturity. Loss of a husband alone did not qualify one for this order.

Although St. Anthony of Egypt is often called the Father of Monasticism, there were people living the monastic life already when he heeded the Lord's words, *If thou wilt be perfect, go and sell that thou hast, and give to the poor, and thou shalt have treasure in heaven: and come and follow Me* (Matthew 19:21). He left his younger sister in the care of "respected and trusted Virgins," and he himself learned from men living the solitary life near his village.

Although not the first monk, St. Anthony's life inspired many to follow in his steps. By the end of the fourth century, the Egyptian desert had become populated with those who had renounced the world in order to seek God.

Those who, like St. Anthony, accept this call of the Lord become the spiritual vanguard of the Church. They remain awake during the watches of the night, praying and keeping vigil while we sleep. They chart

---

[†] Although St. John the Forerunner appears in the pages of the New Testament, he is considered an Old Testament prophet because he died before Christ's death and Resurrection.

the unexplored territory of the human spirit, plumbing the depths of their own sinfulness through their profound, lifelong repentance. They become living examples of life in Christ—vessels of humility from which the pride of this world has been banished through obedience, fasting, and toil.

The Church's daily cycle of prayer is the primary work of the monastic. Monks and nuns spend several hours a day in the temple chanting the Daily Office. Because of our responsibilities in the world, we cannot spend our days in prayer, so monks and nuns spend their days praying for us.

In addition to praying the Daily Office, monks also spend hours in personal prayer, focusing in particular on the Prayer of Jesus. It is in the solitude of his cell that the monk explores the inner regions of his soul, using the Jesus Prayer as his light.

The Jesus Prayer is, above all, a prayer of repentance: "Lord Jesus Christ, Son of God, have mercy on me, *the sinner.*" Repentance is the life of the monk, as Archimandrite George says:

> Repentance is the daily struggle of the monk. His asceticism looks toward this one purpose: that he repent the more deeply and so is more pleasing to God. Repentance is the monk's "science." He does not repent just because he sinned at some time in the past. Rather, he feels intensely and every day that he cannot reply perfectly to God's love. He wants to offer himself completely to God, to be in perfect harmony with His commandments, and not

CHAPTER SEVENTEEN

to embitter Him with the slightest opposition to His will (*The Eros of Repentance*, pp. 16-17).

Notice that Fr. George calls repentance the "science" of the monk. Indeed, monks are the scientists and explorers of the spiritual life. They traverse the inner world of the human spirit, confronting the depths of their own sinfulness as well as the wellsprings of God's infinite grace.

In addition to prayer, the monk has other scientific instruments at his disposal: renunciation, fasting, and obedience. The monk renounces life in the world, giving up all claims to property, inheritance, and even family ties. He does this in order to *lay aside every weight, and the sin which doth so easily beset us* (Hebrews 12:1). The monk takes the admonition of our Lord quite literally:

> *And if thy right hand offend thee, cut it off, and cast it from thee: for it is profitable for thee that one of thy members should perish, and not that thy whole body should be cast into hell* (Matthew 5:30).

In the same way, the monk gives himself over to strenuous fasting, not in order to destroy the body, but to save it. *Man shall not live by bread alone, but by every word that proceedeth out of the mouth of God* (Matthew 4:4). The monk strives to subdue his dependence on the bread of this world in order to lay hold of the Bread of heaven.

Obedience is absolutely central to the monastic life. If prayer is the work of the monk, and repentance his science, then obedience is his tutor and infallible guide.

MONASTICISM

Only through obedience to his spiritual father is the monk's self-will cut off. Only in this way does he grow into the image of His Lord, Who, being God of all, nevertheless prayed, *not My will, but Thine, be done* (Luke 22:42).

It must be stressed that the difference between the life of a monk or nun and that of a layman is one of degree, not kind. All Christians must have as their goal in life the salvation of their souls. All Christians are obliged to pray, fast, and obey the canons of the Church and their spiritual father. Monks, however, renounce life in the world to devote themselves exclusively to the pursuit of salvation, praying for *hours* each day. They fast more strictly and more often than laymen, never eating meat. Furthermore, they are bound to a much deeper level of obedience to their spiritual master.

It is because of their total commitment to life in Christ that monastics live life "on the edge." They experience the life of the Church, both fasts and feasts, in all of its fullness, and they also draw to themselves the attentions of the Evil One and his demons. They are truly the scientists and explorers of the spirit.

As with all sciences, however, some practitioners become more adept than others. The most advanced are called *hesychasts. Hesychia* means "stillness." A hesychast is one who has achieved inner stillness—one who has found the inner place of the heart and dwells there with his God.

Those who excel in virtue become our teachers in the spiritual life. Their experiences—their experiments in the realm of the soul—are recorded in their biogra-

CHAPTER SEVENTEEN

phies and spiritual counsels, as recorded by their disciples. There are thousands upon thousands of pages of such spiritual nourishment available to us today, among them *The Philokalia* and *The Sayings of the Desert Fathers*.

While these books are a great spiritual treasure, the greatest treasure is a living relationship with such a spiritual scientist. It is within such a relationship that the true significance of monasticism becomes apparent. It is when one meets a true monk that one realizes what human life is supposed to be like. Archimandrite Vasileios describes such a man:

> An old monk, a true ascetic comes to our monastery from time to time to ask for a little help. With what he receives, he feeds himself and also helps others, older than himself.... This old man, although he is more than seventy-five, does not expect anyone to respect him. He thinks of himself as a dog. He bows to everyone and asks their blessing, not only to the monks but also to the novices and to the pilgrims who come to us. But he is full of such inexpressible grace that a joyful sense of celebration runs through the monastery every time he comes. All of us, monks and pilgrims, gather round him to hear words of grace which come from his lips, to be encouraged by the joy that his face reflects, without his ever suspecting it. It is like the Father of the desert who asked God that he might not receive any glory on this earth, and whose face was so radiant that no one could look directly at him (*Hymn of Entry*, pp. 123-124).

MONASTICISM
The Fathers Speak

He who has renounced such things as marriage, possessions and other worldly pursuits is outwardly a monk, but may not yet be a monk inwardly. Only he who has renounced the impassioned thoughts of his inner self, which is the intellect, is a true monk. It is easy to be a monk in one's outer self if one wants to be; but no small struggle is required to be a monk in one's inner self.

Who in this generation is completely free from impassioned thoughts and has been granted uninterrupted, pure, and spiritual prayer? Yet this is the mark of the inner monk.

St. Hesychios the Priest
from *On Watchfulness and Holiness*
The Philokalia, vol. 1

The Apostles received this way of life from Christ and made it their own, renouncing the world in response to His call, disregarding fatherland, relatives and possessions. At once they adopted a harsh and strenuous way of life, facing every kind of adversity, afflicted, tormented harassed, naked, lacking even necessities; and finally they met death boldly, imitating their Teacher faithfully in all things. Thus through their actions they left behind a true image of the highest way of life.

St. Neilos the Ascetic
from *Ascetic Discourse*
The Philokalia, vol. 1

CHAPTER SEVENTEEN

Special Study
The Holy Mountain

The spiritual center of Orthodox Christianity is not one of the great cities of the ancient world, but the northern tip of the Chalkidiki Peninsula, jutting into the Aegean Sea: the monastic republic known as Mt. Athos—the Holy Mountain.

The first monastery was established on Mt. Athos by St. Athanasius of Athos in the tenth century. From that time, men flocked to the Holy Mountain to pursue the "angelic life." It is estimated that at one point as many as 40,000 monks lived on the mountain.

At present, more than 1,500 monks live in Athos' twenty ruling monasteries as well as in numerous small skectes and isolated hermitages. If we were to think of the Orthodox Church throughout the world as a single body and of prayer as Her heartbeat, Mt. Athos would be the sinus node that regulates that heartbeat. It is the prayer of these monks on this hallowed rock that sets the rhythm for the spiritual life of the Church.

Mt. Athos is best known to the secular world because women are not permitted anywhere on the mountain. What many people do not realize, however, is that the superior of the Holy Mountain is a woman. According to ancient legend, Mt. Athos was given to the All-holy Theotokos by her Son to be her "garden." This is why Athos is commonly referred to as the "Garden of *Panagia*" (the All-holy One). Thus, the

MONASTICISM

Virgin Mary is the spiritual "abbess" of this all-male monastic republic.

This is quite appropriate, since monasticism itself, whether practiced by monks or nuns, has a certain feminine quality to it. Monasticism has nothing to do with the attainment of worldly power. It is not about control and dominance, but about obedience and contrition of heart: *He hath put down the mighty from their seats, and exalted them of low degree* (Luke 1:52).

Although Mt. Athos has produced scores of bishops and patriarchs, her greatest contribution is the large number of Saints who have lived and died on the Holy Mountain. They have sanctified not only Athos but the entire Church with their lives of prayer and God-centeredness.

St. Gregory Palamas, the defender of Orthodoxy against rationalism and humanism, learned the art of prayer on the Holy Mountain. St. Cosmas the Aitolean was a monk of the Monastery of Philotheou before becoming a missionary preacher.

St. Paisius Velichkovsky spent his time on Mt. Athos collecting the spiritual writings of the Fathers. His work was the foundation for the publication of *The Philokalia* by St. Nicodemos of the Holy Mountain and St. Macarios of Corinth in 1782. St. Paisius translated these works into Slavonic, precipitating a revival of monasiticism in Russia. St. Herman of Alaska, the first Saint of North America, traced his spiritual lineage back to St. Paisius.

Mt. Athos has also produced many God-pleasers in our own century. Perhaps the best known is St. Silouan

CHAPTER SEVENTEEN

(†1938) of St. Panteleimon's Monastery. Silouan was an unlettered Russian peasant who moved to Mt. Athos in 1892 to live out his life in repentance. His repentance was so genuine, his humility so profound, that many came to him for spiritual advice. His chief disciple, Fr. Sophrony (Sakharov), founder of the Monastery of St. John the Baptist in Essex, England, recorded the Saint's spiritual counsels and biography (*The Monk of Mount Athos* and *Wisdom from Mount Athos*).

Another great Saint of twentieth-century Athos, although not nearly as well-known as St. Silouan and not officially canonized, is Elder Joseph the Cave-Dweller (†1954). Elder Joseph was a true hesychast, a man whose entire life was transformed by prayer (Cavrnos, *Anchored in God*, pp. 203-209). His spiritual children have been instrumental in the revival of the spiritual life of Mount Athos over the last thirty years. Through their efforts, Elder Joseph's life and teachings have produced numerous spiritual "grandchildren" throughout the world, including North America.

Although most of us will never have the chance to travel to Mount Athos, the spirit of Athos is present here in North America in the numerous monasteries across the continent. Every Orthodox Christian should take advantage of this great treasure on our shores by making pilgrimages to these monasteries, getting to know the monks and nuns, and by supporting them through our prayers and material gifts. In this way, we too can have a share in the holy work of these spiritual scientists.

MONASTICISM

Reflection

1. Why does St. Paul say that it is preferable not to marry?

2. Is everyone called to live a celibate life?

3. In what way is the celibate life a gift of God?

4. Is marriage evil?

5. What Old Testament figures are the prototypical monks?

6. In what ways are the widows and virgins of the New Testament era the precursors of the monastic life?

7. What is the "science" of the monk?

8. What is a *hesychast*?

9. What is the difference between the spiritual responsibilities of the monk and those of a layman?

10. What is the significance of Mt. Athos in the Orthodox world?

Chapter Eighteen
The Lord's Return

Our Lord Jesus Christ will return to earth in glory, judging all men according to their deeds and establishing His kingdom, which shall have no end.

The Church of Christ lives between the two comings of Christ. At His first advent, the eternal Son and Word of God became man, taking upon Himself the sins of the world and destroying the power of death. At His second advent, He shall come in His heavenly glory, ushering in the end of this age and inaugurating the life of the age to come.

When our Lord ascended to His Father following His Resurrection, two angels appeared to His Disciples as they stood watching:

Ye men of Galilee, why stand ye gazing up into heaven? This same Jesus, Who is taken up from you into heaven, shall so come in like manner as ye have seen Him go into heaven (Acts 1:11).

Since that time the Church has faithfully awaited the return of Her Lord.

The spirit of expectation pervades all that the Church does. We have already noted that Chrismation is the pledge of our future inheritance. We have also

CHAPTER EIGHTEEN

pointed out that the Eucharist is a participation in both Christ's first advent and in the great Wedding Banquet of the kingdom to come: *For as often as ye eat this Bread, and drink this Cup, ye do show the Lord's death till He come* (1 Corinthians 11:26).

Even during the New Testament era, however, this expectation gave rise to strange speculations about the time and details of the Lord's return. Throughout the centuries, many have been led astray by these speculations, departing from the teaching of the Apostles. This is especially true of our own time, in which prophecy "experts" peddle their ideas on television and in popular books and magazines.

It is necessary, therefore, that every Orthodox Christian understand the Church's teaching concerning the Second Coming of Christ. The first thing to remember is that there are very *few* things that the Church states unambiguously concerning our Lord's return. Persons who claim to know intimate details of the Lord's return are deluded.

It is significant that the Book of Revelation (Apocalypse) is the only book of the New Testament that is not read during the Church's services. The Fathers realized that Revelation is a very difficult book, one that is easily misinterpreted. Anyone wishing to know more about the Book of Revelation should begin with the excellent commentary by the late Archbishop Averky (Taushev): *The Apocalypse: In the Teaching of Ancient Christianity.*

Let us, therefore, consider what the Church affirms concerning the Second Coming of Christ and leave

THE LORD'S RETURN

aside those things that our Lord and His Apostles passed over in silence. First of all, the Church affirms that Christ will physically return in glory, although we cannot know the day or the hour. Secondly, when our Lord returns, He will judge every man according to his works. Finally, the Church confesses that Christ's kingdom shall have no end.

Concerning His return in glory, our Lord warned: *But of that day and that hour knoweth no man, no, not the angels which are in heaven, neither the Son, but the Father* (Mark 13:32). How vain it is for us to speculate on the time of Christ's Second Coming! Unfortunately, many have made careers out of doing just that.

The Christians in Thessalonica were making predictions about Christ's return when St. Paul rebuked them:

> *Let no man deceive you by any means: for that Day shall not come, except there come a falling away first, and that Man of Sin be revealed, the Son of Perdition; who opposeth and exalteth himself above all that is called God, or that is worshipped; so that he as God sitteth in the temple of God, showing himself that he is God* (2 Thessalonians 2:3-4).

According to St. Paul, two events will precede the Second Coming. First of all, there will be a general falling away, or apostasy, from the truth. Our Lord asked, *When the Son of Man cometh, shall He find faith on the earth* (Luke 18:8)? Mankind will become more sinful as the end of the age approaches, and many will leave the Church to follow their own desires.

The second event is the revelation of the Antichrist. The word *Antichrist* literally means "instead of Christ."

CHAPTER EIGHTEEN

The Antichrist will not present himself as an ugly, malevolent being, but as a caring savior. He and his minions will perform miracles and solve great social problems, winning the allegiance of many Christians:

> *Then if any man shall say unto you, "Lo, here is Christ, or there;" believe it not. For there shall arise false Christs, and false prophets, and shall show great signs and wonders; insomuch that, if it were possible, they shall deceive the very Elect* (Matthew 24:23-24).

Only after he has won the allegiance of the world will the Antichrist reveal his true self, and the period of great tribulation shall begin:

> *For then shall be great tribulation, such as was not since the beginning of the world to this time, no, nor ever shall be. And except those days should be shortened, there should no flesh be saved: but for the Elect's sake those days shall be shortened* (Matthew 24:21-22).

There is a teaching popular among Evangelical Protestants that asserts that Christians will be miraculously delivered from the tribulation and that only the "unsaved" will suffer under the rule of the Antichrist. The idea that Christians will be "raptured" — that is, taken up into heaven — before the tribulation is an invention of the nineteenth century. No one in the previous 1800 years of Church history ever came up with such a notion.

Our Lord made it perfectly clear that the period of tribulation will be shortened precisely for the sake of the Elect (cf. Matthew 24:22). That is why we are told to

THE LORD'S RETURN

watch and stand fast in the faith, so that we will not be deceived.

It is no accident that the "Rapture" is often paired with the idea of a worldwide revival before the Second Coming. Thus, many Christians are expecting a new outpouring of the Holy Spirit with great miracles and mass conversions before the Church is taken up to heaven.

We know from the Divine Scriptures, however, that this is the exact opposite of what will happen. There will, of course, be a great revival, complete with signs and wonders. This will be the deception of the Antichrist. Those who are expecting to be delivered *before* the advent of the Antichrist will be ill-prepared to recognize him. It is obvious that Satan himself is the author of the "Rapture" myth; it is part of the Antichrist's campaign of deception.

Our task as Orthodox Christians is not to try to predict the future but to watch and pray. We are to be as the wise virgins in the parable, who had their lamps filled with oil in expectation of the Bridegroom's call (cf. Matthew 25:1-13). We must be prepared, for when our Lord appears, we shall stand before His Throne of Judgment and give an account of our lives.

The second major point that the Church affirms about the Second Coming of Christ is that He is coming to render final judgment. Everyone who has ever lived will come before Him:

> [God] *will render to every man according to his deeds: To them who by patient continuance in well doing seek for glory and honor and immortality, eternal life. But*

CHAPTER EIGHTEEN

unto them that are contentious, and do not obey the truth, but obey unrighteousness, indignation and wrath, tribulation and anguish, upon every soul of man that doeth evil, of the Jew first, and also of the Gentile; but glory, honor, and peace, to every man that worketh good, to the Jew first, and also to the Gentile (Romans 2:6-10).

There is another false teaching popular among Evangelical Protestants that says that Christians will be exempt from this judgment. Do not be led astray by such nonsense. *All* of us will be called before Christ to give an account of our lives. That is why at every Liturgy we pray for "a Christian ending to our life, painless, unashamed, and peaceful, and for a good defense before the dread Judgment Seat of Christ."

When Christ returns, the dead shall rise, the books shall be opened, and men shall be sent to their eternal destinies. The righteous shall reign together with Christ in His kingdom—a kingdom that shall have no end. This is the third point that the Church affirms concerning Christ's Second Coming.

In the early Church a heresy arose concerning the nature of Christ's kingdom. Misinterpreting the statement in Revelation, *and they lived and reigned with Christ a thousand years* (20:4), many began to teach that Christ would rule an earthly kingdom for one thousand years before the final consummation of the age. This teaching was condemned as heresy by the Second Ecumenical Council, and the phrase "Whose kingdom shall have no end" was added to the Creed.

God created the world in six days, and on the seventh day He rested. The millennial reign of Christ is the

THE LORD'S RETURN

seventh day. This is the age of the Church. We, who have been united with Christ in Baptism and anointed with the Holy Spirit, live and reign with Him here and now.

The Book of Revelation speaks of two deaths and two resurrections. The first death is our physical death, the second death is the eternal death of hell. The first resurrection is our spiritual resurrection accomplished at Baptism. The second resurrection is the general resurrection of all the dead. St. John writes:

Blessed and holy is he that hath part in the first resurrection: on such the second death hath no power, but they shall be priests of God and of Christ, and shall reign with Him a thousand years (Revelation 20:6).

Those who experience the first resurrection will die physically, but they will be raised again to live in eternal life with God. Those, however, who have no part in the first resurrection will be raised again only to undergo the second death, which is hell.

We live in the seventh day, but when Christ returns a new Day will dawn—not the first day of a new cycle, but the Eighth and final Day, the Day that knows no end. Creation as we know it will be transformed; all will be transfigured by the power of Christ's Resurrection and the divine life of the All-holy Trinity. There shall be a new heaven and a new earth, *and God shall wipe away all tears from their eyes . . . for the former things are passed away* (Revelation 21:4).

CHAPTER EIGHTEEN

THE FATHERS SPEAK

Blessed is the man who, in the day of God's just Judgment, when the Lord comes to "throw light on the hidden things, of the darkness, and to reveal the intentions of men's hearts," submits boldly to that testing light, and comes out unashamed because his conscience is unpolluted by evil actions. While those who have acted wickedly will "rise to reproach and shame," for they will see in themselves their disgrace, and the marks of their sins. . . . For they will have always before their eyes the evidence of their sins committed in the flesh, like some indelible stain, which will endure in the memory of their souls for all eternity.

St. Basil the Great
from *Homilies on the Psalms*
The Later Christian Fathers

How shall it be in that Hour and fearful Day, when the Judge shall sit on His dread Throne! The books shall be opened and men's actions shall be examined, and the secrets of darkness shall be made public. . . . Come ye and hearken, kings and princes, slaves and free, sinners and righteous, rich and poor: for the Judge comes to pass sentence on the whole inhabited earth. And who shall bear to stand before His face in the presence of the angels, as they call us to account of our actions and our thoughts, whether by night or by day? How shall it be then in that Hour? But before the end is here, make haste my soul, and cry: "O God Who only art compassionate, turn me back and save me."

from *The Lenten Triodion*

THE LORD'S RETURN
Special Study
Heaven and Hell

The Divine Scriptures state explicitly that we will be judged by Christ and not by God the Father: *For the Father judgeth no man, but hath committed all judgment unto the Son* (John 5:22). We will be judged by the One Who took upon Himself our humanity and lived a perfect human life. Christ's life is the standard against which our lives will be measured.

Our Lord said that when He returns He will separate mankind into two groups, as a shepherd separates the sheep from the goats. The sheep will inherit the kingdom of God, while the goats will inherit the everlasting fire prepared for the devil. What is most interesting about his parable is the criteria for the judgment:

> *"Come, ye blessed of My Father, inherit the kingdom prepared for you from the foundation of the world: For I was hungry, and ye gave Me food. I was thirsty, and ye gave Me drink. I was a stranger, and ye took Me in; naked, and ye clothed Me. I was sick, and ye visited Me. I was in prison, and ye came unto Me." Then shall the righteous answer Him, saying, "Lord, when saw we Thee hungry, and fed Thee? or thirsty, and gave Thee drink? . . ." And the King shall answer and say unto them, "Verily I say unto you, inasmuch as ye have done it unto one of the least of these My brethren, ye have done it unto Me"* (Matthew 25:34-40).

Not only is each and every human being created in the image of God, but, because of the Incarnation, every

CHAPTER EIGHTEEN

human being is a blood brother of Christ Himself. How we relate to others determines to how we relate to God.

This insight into the nature of the Last Judgment also provides us with an insight into the nature of heaven and hell. We must not be misled into thinking of heaven and hell in purely materialistic terms—simply as "places" of reward or punishment. We must also consider the spiritual reality of heaven and hell.

When Christ returns, heaven and earth will pass away, and there will be a new heaven and a new earth. We cannot say exactly what this new creation will be like, for *eye hath not seen, nor ear heard, neither have entered into the heart of man, the things which God hath prepared for them that love Him* (1 Corinthians 2:9).

The new creation will be material in some sense, but not in the sense that we understand matter in this life. The most we can say is that it will be like our Lord's resurrected body. It could be touched and handled, yet it was not bound by space or the laws of nature as we know them.

It is, therefore, a heresy to say that the kingdom to come is purely immaterial. If that were the case, there would be no point in the universal resurrection. It is equally dangerous, however, to overemphasize the material nature of the kingdom. What point would there be in living in a glorious palace if one's soul were unfit to enjoy its treasures? On the other hand, what flames could possibly torture one whose heart is full of love?

When Christ returns in glory *and when all things shall be subdued unto Him, then shall the Son also Himself be subject unto Him that put all things under Him, that God may be all in all* (1 Corinthians 15:28). God's immediate presence will be to those who love Him the very bliss of heaven, and to those who hate Him the very fire of hell. "The fire of hell," said one of the Desert Fathers, "is the love of God."

We have said that man is created in the image of the Holy Trinity to live his life in an eternal communion of love with God, his fellow men, and the whole created order. Those who, through union with Christ and the power of the Holy Spirit, attain *to the measure of the stature of the fulness of Christ* (Ephesians 4:13), will enter into the joy of their Lord. They will experience His presence as love and peace and eternal joy, for they shall be like Him (1 John 3:2).

On the other hand, those who prefer their self-contained individuality, exulting in their slavery to the passions, will rise from the grave only to be confronted by the One Who is the eternal antithesis of their spiritual disposition. Those for whom "hell is other people" (Sartre) will stand before the Eternal Other. His love will condemn their hatred. His selflessness will condemn their self-centeredness. His gift of eternal life will be their curse of eternal death, and they will take their place with their spiritual kindred, Satan and his angels. Let us, therefore, pray and work that we will be numbered with the sheep and not the goats!

CHAPTER EIGHTEEN

Reflection

1. What did the two angels promise the Apostles as Christ ascended to heaven?

2. What is the only book of the New Testament that is not read liturgically in Church?

3. When did Christ say He would return?

4. What two things will happen before Christ returns?

5. Will the spiritual climate of the world get better or worse before Christ returns?

6. What does the word *Antichrist* mean?

7. Will Christians be exempted from the tribulation?

8. How long will Christ's kingdom last?

9. Will Christians be exempted from the Last Judgment?

10. What is the nature of heaven and hell?

Conclusion
Living an Orthodox Life in a Secular World

To be faithful Orthodox Christians, we must live according to the light that God has given us and share that light with the world.

Being an Orthodox Christian is the greatest privilege in the world. We have been entrusted with the most beautiful treasure: the truth about God, about the world, and about ourselves. We have the writings of the holy Fathers and the counsels of grace-filled monks and nuns to guide us. We have the opportunity to stand before God, our Creator, and worship Him in Spirit and in Truth, receiving from Him the very life of the Holy Trinity.

> *Let them praise the name of the* LORD: *for His name alone is excellent; His glory is above the earth and heaven. He also exalteth the horn of His people, the praise of all His Saints; even of the Children of Israel, a people near unto Him. Praise ye the* LORD (Psalm 148:13-14).

With great privilege, however, comes great responsibility, for *unto whomsoever much is given, of him shall be much required* (Luke 12:48). Each of us will stand before

CONCLUSION

the Throne of God and give an account of our life. We will be judged according to the light we have been given. We cannot say what will happen to those who have never heard the name of Christ or who have heard the Gospel preached only in a partial or heretical form. We *do* know, however, that we who have received the Gospel in all of its fullness will be held accountable for it.

The holy Apostles command us to hold fast to the faith that we have received and to live according to it: *Therefore, brethren, stand fast, and hold the traditions which ye have been taught, whether by word, or our epistle* (2 Thessalonians 2:15).

What great perdition awaits those who change the faith: *But though we, or an angel from heaven, preach any other Gospel unto you than that which we have preached unto you, let him be accursed* (Galatians 1:8). Hear also the words of our Savior: *And whosoever shall offend one of these little ones that believe in Me, it is better for him that a millstone were hanged about his neck, and he were cast into the sea* (Mark 9:42). We are to guard the faith which has been entrusted to us, changing *nothing*.

It is not enough, however, merely to preserve the faith. Those who confess the Orthodox Faith yet fail to live Orthodox lives will face the greatest condemnation of all. What excuse will we offer to the Lord, our Judge, when we stand before Him? We cannot claim that we did not know the truth. We cannot claim that we were not taught the ways of righteousness. The very gift of Orthodoxy will serve to condemn us on that Day if we fail to live according to the Gospel:

LIVING AN ORTHODOX LIFE

Not every one that saith unto Me, "Lord, Lord," shall enter into the kingdom of heaven; but he that doeth the will of My Father Who is in heaven. Many will say to Me in that day, "Lord, Lord, have we not prophesied in Thy name? and in Thy name have cast out devils? and in Thy name done many wonderful works?" And then will I profess unto them, "I never knew you: depart from Me, ye that work iniquity." Therefore whosoever heareth these sayings of Mine, and doeth them, I will liken him unto a wise man, which built his house upon a rock: And the rain descended, and the floods came, and the winds blew, and beat upon that house; and it fell not: for it was founded upon a rock. And every one that heareth these sayings of Mine, and doeth them not, shall be likened unto a foolish man, which built his house upon the sand: And the rain descended, and the floods came, and the winds blew, and beat upon that house; and it fell: and great was the fall of it (Matthew 7:21-27).

The Secular World

Living an Orthodox life is easier said than done, however. We do not live in the Christian Roman Empire or in pre-Revolutionary Russia, where social life was built around the Church. Our situation is much more akin to that of Christians before the conversion of Constantine, when Christianity was an illicit, often persecuted, religion.

Although our society still exhibits vestiges of a "Christian culture," this is deceiving. The idea of a "Christian America" is a myth, similar to the romantic portrayals of the Old South in the movies. The presence

CONCLUSION

of beautiful, antebellum mansions does nothing to erase the fact that it was a society built on slavery.

The founding fathers of the United States were, for the most part, Deists and Masons. In addition to writing the Declaration of Independence, Thomas Jefferson also compiled his own "Bible"—an expurgated version of the Gospels in which all of the miracle stories were omitted. Such stories had no place in Jefferson's rationalistic worldview. This was the architect of American Democracy.

The intellectual foundation of American society was the Enlightenment and its exaltation of human reason above faith. To be sure, Americans have generally been very conservative socially, and public morality has, until recently, borne the distinctive marks of Protestant Christianity. It was inevitable, however, that this edifice of Christian morals would be washed away by the tide of rationalism, like a sandcastle doomed by its proximity to the sea.

Modern society is, at best, indifferent, and often hostile, to Christianity. It is a dogma of our society that man is nothing more than an evolved animal. The Bible is an ancient book, no different from other ancient books, full of superstitions. Traditional Christianity is nothing more than a male-dominated power structure that denies equal rights to women and minorities.

Christian morals fare no better. Greed and gluttony are a way of life, perversions are considered normal, and, worst of all, millions of unborn children are murdered each year in the name of convenience and "women's rights."

LIVING AN ORTHODOX LIFE

Surely a truly Orthodox life in the modern world is very difficult, but we must not despair: *Lo, I am with you always, even unto the end of the world.* (Matthew 28:20). And again: *With men this is impossible; but with God all things are possible* (Matthew 19:26).

Strategies for Godly Living

Although living a Christian life in this world is difficult, it is not impossible. Here are some strategies for Godly living:

The most important element in remaining faithful to the Gospel of Christ is the *commitment* to do so. We must firmly resolve to take up our Cross and follow our Lord. Be assured: the devil will test our resolve. But *let us not be weary in well doing: for in due season we shall reap, if we faint not* (Galatians 6:9).

The strength of our commitment, however, will only be as strong as the strength of our faith. Modern Christianity is spiritually anemic because the faith of modern man has been eroded by rationalism. If we are to remain steadfast in our commitment to Christ, we must be strong in our faith.

Orthodoxy is truly a great banquet, but it is not a *buffet*. We cannot pick and choose those elements of the faith we will believe and those we will ignore. We are not free to underline our favorite Bible verses, while we disregard those verses that make us uncomfortable. On the contrary, we are to become as little children and accept the faith which has been transmitted to us joyfully and without reserve:

CONCLUSION

And Jesus called a little child unto Him, and set him in the midst of them, and said, "Verily I say unto you, Except ye be converted, and become as little children, ye shall not enter into the kingdom of heaven. Whosoever therefore shall humble himself as this little child, the same is greatest in the kingdom of heaven" (Matthew 18:2-4).

Once we have resolved with all our heart and all our strength to live life according to the Gospel, the next important step is to establish and *keep* a daily rule of prayer. Prayer is our primary source of spiritual strength and our first line of defense against the attacks of the devil. Without prayer, living a Christian life is hopeless; with prayer, we are assured of the help of God:

Be careful for nothing; but in every thing by prayer and supplication with thanksgiving let your requests be made known unto God. And the peace of God, which passeth all understanding, shall keep your hearts and minds through Christ Jesus (Philippians 4:6-7).

The next most important strategy in living a Christian life is to have a relationship with a spiritual father. Accountability is essential to spiritual growth. Not only do we receive the forgiveness of our sins through sacramental Confession, our relationship with our spiritual father provides encouragement and direction for our lives.

In addition to this, we must make every effort to attend the Divine Services of the Church. Attendance at Saturday Vespers (or Vigil) and Sunday Matins and Liturgy is the bare minimum. We must be willing to sacrifice our leisure time activities in order to participate in the fasts and feasts of the Church. Many Orthodox Christians use their vacation time in order to attend the services of Holy Week, especially Great and Holy Friday. This is truly a pious act. How shall we stand before Christ, Who gave His life for us, if we cannot make room in our busy schedules to worship Him and receive the gifts of grace that He offers to us?

Another useful strategy is to make frequent pilgrimages to monasteries. At monasteries we can experience a fuller liturgical cycle than that available in our local parishes. Furthermore, we can take advantage of the peace and solitude that they afford the pilgrim, participating, if only for a time, in the monastic's rhythm of life.

While pilgrimages and retreats are beneficial to the soul, there are also ways in which we can make our daily lives more peaceful. One of the best strategies is to limit the amount of television we watch. Many families have even eliminated television altogether. *He that hath ears to hear, let him hear* (Matthew 11:15).

Our eyes and ears are the doorways to our soul. There is no way we can keep our minds and bodies pure while we constantly gaze upon and listen to suggestive programming and music. The problem is not so much the pornography sold in adult bookstores as the seemingly innocuous popular entertainments which fill our leisure time.

From soap operas, situation comedies, and afternoon talk shows, our children are taught that premarital and extramarital sex is acceptable. They learn to imi-

CONCLUSION

tate the irreverent and beastly behavior of their heroes. From "educational television" they learn that Christianity is a man-made religion like all the others and that human intelligence will one day solve all of man's problems.

Guarding the windows to our soul is not only necessary for *our* salvation, it is especially necessary for the salvation of our families. *Train up a child in the way he should go: and when he is old, he will not depart from it* (Proverbs 22:6).

Unfortunately, in our society parents must be as wary of what goes on in the schools as they are of what their children see on television. Many parents are opting to teach their children at home so that they can be sure that their children receive a quality education and training in righteousness. Whether home schooling is an option or not, all parents must take an active role in their children's education, reading their textbooks and discussing with them what they are learning in school. In this way, parents can regain at least some control over their children's intellectual formation.

This is not to suggest that we must withdraw completely from the popular culture. Indeed, exposure to the arts is essential to a well-rounded education. The key is discernment. There is plenty of good, edifying literature and popular entertainment available, but we must learn to separate the wheat from the chaff.

In all of this we must have one, and only one, goal in mind: the salvation of our soul and of our family. We do not pray for the sake of prayer, attend services in order to get a good attendance certificate, or turn off the television just for the sake of a little peace and quiet. We do these things so that we may obtain a crown that is incorruptible—so that we may be conformed to the image of Christ, participating in the communion of love which is the life of the Holy Trinity:

> *Moreover when ye fast, be not, as the hypocrites, of a sad countenance: for they disfigure their faces, that they may appear unto men to fast. Verily I say unto you, They have their reward. But thou, when thou fastest, anoint thine head, and wash thy face; that thou appear not unto men to fast, but unto thy Father Who is in secret: and thy Father, Who seeth in secret, shall reward thee openly. Lay not up for yourselves treasures upon earth, where moth and rust doth corrupt, and where thieves break through and steal: But lay up for yourselves treasures in heaven, where neither moth nor rust doth corrupt, and where thieves do not break through nor steal: For where your treasure is, there will your heart be also* (Matthew 6:16-21).

Social Engagement

The idea of catacomb Christianity has a certain romantic appeal to it. It is easy to picture ourselves as a persecuted minority, meeting in secret and living a life of inner rebellion against a world which has sold itself to the devil. Indeed, this *is* what will happen during the reign of the Antichrist. Nevertheless, the end of the age, however close at hand it may be, is not here *yet*.

Until the time comes when Christians can no longer live their faith openly, we have a duty to engage the so-

CONCLUSION

ciety in which we live and bear witness to the light that is within us:

> *Ye are the light of the world. A city that is set on an hill cannot be hid. Neither do men light a candle, and put it under a bushel, but on a candlestick; and it giveth light unto all that are in the house. Let your light so shine before men, that they may see your good works, and glorify your Father Who is in heaven* (Matthew 5:14-16).

Although our society is in many ways like that of the Roman Empire before the conversion of Constantine, there is one major difference: We have a voice in how our government is run and in how our society is structured. Orthodox Christians must make their voices heard.

The first and most fundamental rule of Orthodox social engagement is that we are to judge *no one*. This is a difficult challenge. When we are faced with manifest evil and all manner of sexual perversions, it is difficult not to feel in some sense superior to those living their lives in sin. Nevertheless, we must remember that our own souls are as full of evil desires as anyone, and that *we* will be judged with the same measure with which we judge others:

> *And even as they did not like to retain God in their knowledge, God gave them over to a reprobate mind, to do those things which are not convenient; being filled with all unrighteousness, fornication, wickedness, covetousness, maliciousness; full of envy, murder, debate, deceit, malignity; whisperers, backbiters, haters of God, despiteful, proud, boasters, inventors of evil things, disobedient to parents, without understanding, covenantbreak-*

ers, without natural affection, implacable, unmerciful: Who knowing the judgment of God, that they which commit such things are worthy of death, not only do the same, but have pleasure in them that do them. Therefore thou art inexcusable, O man, whosoever thou art that judgest: For wherein thou judgest another, thou condemnest thyself; for thou that judgest doest the same things. But we are sure that the judgment of God is according to truth against them which commit such things. And thinkest thou this, O man, that judgest them which do such things, and doest the same, that thou shalt escape the judgment of God (Romans 1:28-2:3)?

Keeping this in mind, let us consider several social concerns and some ways in which we, as Orthodox Christians, can address them: (1) environmental issues; (2) social justice; (3) abortion; and (4) public morality.

Let us begin with the very ground on which we stand. We have said that the proper relationship with the world is a sacramental one. We receive the things of this world as a *gift of communion* from God, and we must use them with respect and care. Proper stewardship of the world begins with conservation in our homes and can extend to active support of conservation organizations.

Recycling aluminum cans and newspapers is a simple and painless way to begin caring for our environment. From there we can move to participation in community clean-up programs. We can also work to ensure that our places of employment are sensitive to environmental concerns. Finally, we should be aware of legislation that affects the environment, and we should let our representatives know our opinions.

CONCLUSION

As beautiful as a mountain stream or a forest is, however, the whole of creation is not as valuable as *one* human being, for every person sums up within himself the entirety of the human race and is the very image of his Creator. When we encounter a street person, a derelict, or a hungry child, we must remember that we are encountering our very selves.

Poverty, hunger, and injustice are *our* problems, because they affect our brethren. We must participate fully in the charitable efforts of our local parish and diocese. We can also participate in local community efforts such as food banks and clothing closets. One of the simplest things we can do is to take the time to visit nursing homes, sharing our love with those who have been forgotten by the world.

It is important to note, however, that there is no single Christian position in regard to the exact role which government should play in dealing with many social problems. It is possible for Orthodox Christians to take different sides of a given public debate on some issues. Neither the Democratic nor the Republican Party can claim to represent the "Christian" position on all social issues.

There is one social issue, however, about which there can be no discussion and no compromise: the abortion holocaust. The Church has condemned abortion as murder from the very beginning. This is not up for debate.

No Orthodox Christian may have an abortion or in any way help or encourage someone else to have an abortion. No Orthodox Christian medical professional may perform or assist in performing abortions. In addition, it is unconscionable for an Orthodox Christian to belong to such demonic organizations as the National Organization for Woman or Planned Parenthood.

Why is the position of the Church on abortion so intransigent? Because we believe in the Holy Trinity! We believe that God is a personal being Whose very life and essence is love. We believe that we are created in the image of this God of Triune Love—that each person is unique and unrepeatable, summing up within himself all of humanity. We also believe that God has become man, uniting humanity with Himself, becoming our Brother as well as our Lord. The murder of one child by abortion is, therefore, an act of genocide and, by extension, an act of deicide: *Inasmuch as ye have done it unto one of the least of these My brethren, ye have done it unto Me* (Matthew 25:40).

While supporting local pro-life organizations and using our vote to influence public policy is important, it is even more important that we work to create alternatives to abortion. Crisis pregnancy centers and Christian adoption programs desperately need our support.

Most important of all, if we are to stop the abortion holocaust, we must show the world a better way to live. Abortion is a grave sin because it is a refusal to love. The eyes of abortion see a child as a problem to be solved rather than as a gift of God, given for our salvation. We must share *our* vision of reality with the world around us.

As with all sin, the greatest victim is the one who commits it. In the case of abortion, the greatest victim is

CONCLUSION

the mother. In murdering her child, she has murdered her own soul. We must reach out to these victims of abortion, and to those who may yet be victimized, and share with them the unconditional love of the Holy Trinity. Only when *we* begin to experience the Trinitarian life of the Church and share that life with the world around us will we put a stop to abortion.

Allowing the light and life of the All-holy Trinity to shine through our life into the world around us is also the way we must address issues of public morality. We can no longer expect the government to be the guardian of public mores. *We* must be the light of the world.

There are some concrete things, of course, that we can do to influence society. We can refuse to patronize stores which sell pornographic literature. We can refuse to spend our money on music and movies which encourage unrighteousness.

In the final analysis, however, it is how *we* live *our* lives that is influential. There is no point in decrying the divorce rate or sexual promiscuity when we are not working to make our own homes into genuine Christian homes. The world is in darkness, searching for truth and light; if *we* are not bearers of truth and light, the world will remain in darkness.

To live an Orthodox life in our society is not something that we can accomplish on our own. The glorious truth of Orthodoxy, however, is that we are *not alone*. The life to which we are called is lived within the Church, which is Christ's Body, *the fullness of Him that filleth all in all*. The life we live in Christ is life in the Holy Trinity.

LIVING AN ORTHODOX LIFE

May the All-Holy Trinity, through the intercessions of our Sovereign Lady Theotokos and of all the Saints who have been well-pleasing unto Him throughout the ages, grant us His grace to faithfully live the life to which we have been called, and the boldness to share that life with the world.

> Such is the life in Christ, concealed, and thus made manifest by the light of good works, which is love. In love the brightness of all virtue consists and, as far as human effort is concerned, it constitutes the life in Christ. Accordingly one would not err by calling it life, for it is union with God. This union is life, just as we know that death is separation from God. For this reason Christ says, *His commandment is eternal life* (John 12:50). Speaking of love the Savior also says, *the words that I speak to you are spirit and life* (John 6:63), of which love is the sum, and *he who abides in love abides in God and God in him* (1 John 4:16), which is the same as abiding in life and life in him, for He says, *I am the life* (John 11:25, 14:6). . . . What then may life be more fittingly called than love? For that which alone survives and does not allow the living to die when all things have been taken away is life—and such is love. When all things have passed away in the age to come as Paul says (1 Corinthians 13:8,10), love remains, and it alone suffices for life in Christ Jesus our Lord, to Whom is due all glory forever. Amen (St. Nicholas Cabasilas, *The Life in Christ*).

RECOMMENDED READING

The following books are recommended for further study. Books in the "Beginning" category are especially suited for those with little previous knowledge of Orthodoxy. Most readers of this volume will be able to profit from the books listed in the "Intermediate" category. Books in the "Advanced" category deal with advanced levels of theology and spirituality and should be read by those who have first gained a sound understanding of the Church's theology and prayer life. Books listed in bold type are especially recommended.

Beginning

Gillquist, Peter E. *Becoming Orthodox: A Journey to the Ancient Christian Faith.* Ben Lomond, CA: Conciliar Press, 1992.

Gillquist, Peter E., Ed. *Coming Home: Why Protestant Clergy are Becoming Orthodox.* Ben Lomond, CA: Conciliar Press, 1992.

Hopko, Thomas. *The Orthodox Faith: An Elementary Handbook on the Orthodox Church.* 4 Vols. New York: Department of Religious Education (OCA), 1981.

Irenaios of Lyons, St. *The Preaching of the Apostles.* Tr. by Jack N. Sparks. Brookline, MA: Holy Cross Orthodox Press, 1987.

RECOMMENDED READING

Nieuwsma, Virginia, Ed. *Our Hearts True Home: Fourteen Warm, Inspiring Stories of Women Discovering the Ancient Christian Faith.* Ben Lomond, CA: Conciliar Press, 1996.

Rose, Seraphim. *God's Revelation to the Human Heart.* Platina, CA: St. Herman of Alaska Brotherhood, 1987.

Ware, Kallistos (Timothy). *The Orthodox Church.* New York: Penguin Books, 1984.

_____. *The Orthodox Way.* Crestwood, NY: St. Vladimir's Seminary Press, 1995.

Intermediate

Aleksiev, Seraphim. *The Forgotten Medicine: The Mystery of Repentance.* Tr. by Ralitsa Doynova. Wildwood, CA: St. Xenia Scete Press, 1994.

_____. *The Meaning of Suffering* and *Strife and Reconciliation.* Tr. by Ralitsa Doynova. Wildwood, CA: St. Xenia Scete Press, 1994.

Athanasius of Alexandria, St. *On the Incarnation.* Crestwood, NY: St. Vladimir's Seminary Press, 1982.

Basil of Caesarea, St. *On the Holy Spirit.* Tr. by David Anderson. Crestwood, NY: St. Vladimir's Seminary Press, 1980.

Bettenson, Henry, Ed. *The Early Christian Fathers.* New York: Oxford University Press, 1969.

RECOMMENDED READING

_____. *The Later Christian Fathers.* New York: Oxford University Press, 1972.

Cabasilas, St. Nicholas. *The Life in Christ.* **Tr. by Carmino J. deCatanzaro. Crestwood, NY: St. Vladimir's Seminary Press, 1974.**

Capsanis, George. *The Eros of Repentance.* Tr. by Alexander Golitzen. Newbury, MA: Praxis Institute Press.

Cavarnos, Constantine. *Anchored in God.* Belmont, MA: Institute for Byzantine and Modern Greek Studies, 1975.

_____. *The Holy Mountain.* Belmont, MA: Institute for Byzantine and Modern Greek Studies, 1973.

Chondropoulos, Sotos. *Saint Nektarios: A Saint for our Times.* Tr. by Peter and Aliki Los. Brookline: Holy Cross Orthodox Press, 1989.

Cyril of Jerusalem, St. *Lectures on the Christian Sacraments.* Ed. by F. L. Cross. Crestwood, NY: St. Vladimir's Seminary Press, 1986.

Dmitri, Archbishop. *The Kingdom of God: The Sermon on the Mount.* **Crestwood, NY: St. Vladimir's Seminary Press, 1992.**

_____. *The Parables.* **Crestwood, NY: St. Vladimir's Seminary Press, 1996.**

Engleman, Dennis E. *Ultimate Things: An Orthodox Christian Perspective on the End Times.* Ben Lomond, CA: Conciliar Press, 1995.

RECOMMENDED READING

Holy Transfiguration Monastery, Tr. *The Pentecostarion.* Boston, MA: Holy Transfiguration Monastery, 1990.

John Chrysostom, St. *On Marriage and Family Life.* Tr. by Catharine P. Roth and David Anderson. Crestwood, NY: St. Vladimir's Seminary Press, 1986.

_____. *On Wealth and Poverty.* Tr. by Catharine P. Roth. Crestwood, NY: St. Vladimir's Seminary Press, 1984.

John of Damascus, St. *On the Divine Images.* Tr. by David Anderson. Crestwood, NY: St. Vladimir's Seminary Press, 1980.

Karambelas, Cherubim. *Contemporary Ascetics of Mt. Athos.* 2 Vols. Platina, CA: St. Herman of Alaska Brotherhood, 1991.

Mary, Mother and Kallistos Timothy Ware, Trs. *The Festal Menaion.* London: Faber and Faber, 1969.

_____. *The Lenten Triodion.* London: Faber and Faber, 1978.

Maretta, Thomas, Tr. *The Great Collection of the Lives of the Saints.* 12 Volumes in progress. House Springs, MO: Chrysostom Press, 1994-.

Maximovitch, St. John. *The Orthodox Veneration of Mary the Birthgiver of God.* Tr. by Seraphim Rose. Platina, CA: St. Herman of Alaska Brotherhood, 1994.

Meyendorff, John. *Byzantine Theology: Historical Trends and Doctrinal Themes.* New York: Fordham University Press, 1983.

RECOMMENDED READING

Oleksa, Michael. *Orthodox Alaska: A Theology of Mission.* Crestwood, NY: St. Vladimir's Seminary Press, 1992.

Ouspensky, Leonid and Vladimir Lossky. *The Meaning of Icons.* Tr. by G.E.H. Palmer and E. Kadloubovsky. Crestwood, NY: St. Vladimir's Seminary Press, 1983.

Perekrestov, Peter, Ed. *Man of God: Saint John of Shanghai and San Francisco.* Redding, CA: Nikodemus Orthodox Publication Society, 1994.

Pomazansky, Michael. *Orthodox Dogmatic Theology: A Concise Exposition.* Tr. by Seraphim Rose. Platina, CA: St. Herman of Alaska Brotherhood, 1994.

Quenot, Michel. *The Icon: Window on the Kingdom.* Crestwood, NY: St. Vladimir's Seminary Press, 1991.

Sakharov, Sophrony. *The Monk of Mount Athos: Staretz Silouan 1866-1938.* Tr. by Rosemary Edmonds. Crestwood, NY: St. Vladimir's Seminary Press, 1975.

_____. *Wisdom from Mount Athos: The Writings of Staretz Silouan 1866-1938.* Tr. by Rosemary Edmonds. Crestwood, NY: St. Vladimir's Seminary Press, 1975.

Schaeffer, Frank. *Dancing Alone: The Quest for Orthodox Faith in the Age of False Religion.* Brookline: Holy Cross Orthodox Press, 1994.

RECOMMENDED READING

———. *Letters to Father Aristotle: A Journey Through Contemporary American Orthodoxy.* Salisbury, MA: Regina Orthodox Press, 1995.

Schmemann, Alexander. *Great Lent: Journey to Pascha.* Crestwood, NY: St. Vladimir's Seminary Press, 1974.

Symeon the New Theologian, St. *The First-Created Man.* Tr. by Seraphim Rose. Platina, CA: St. Herman of Alaska Brotherhood, 1994.

———. *On the Mystical Life.* 3 Vols. Tr. by Alexander Golitzen. Crestwood, NY: St. Vladimir's Seminary Press, 1995-.

Taushev, Averky. *The Apocalypse: In the Teaching of Ancient Christianity.* Tr. by Seraphim Rose. Platina, CA: St. Herman of Alaska Brotherhood, 1995.

Theodore the Studite, St. *On the Holy Icons.* Tr. by Catharine P. Roth. Crestwood, NY: St. Vladimir's Seminary Press, 1981.

Theophan the Recluse, St. *The Spiritual Life: And How to be Attuned to It.* Tr. by Alexandra Dockham. Platina, CA: St. Herman of Alaska Brotherhood, 1995.

Theophylact of Ochrid. *Blessed Theophylact's Explanation of the New Testament.* 4 Vols. House Springs, MO: Chrysostom Press, 1993-.

Vlachos, Hierotheos. *The Illness and Cure of the Soul in the Orthodox Tradition.* Tr. by Effie Mavromichali. Levadia, Greece: Birth of the Theotokos Monastery, 1993.

RECOMMENDED READING

Ward, Benedicta, Tr. *The Sayings of the Desert Fathers: The Alphabetical Collection.* Kalamazoo, MI: Cistercian Publications, 1975.

Advanced

Cassian, St. John. *Conferences.* Tr. by Colm Luibheid. In *The Classics of Western Spirituality.* New York: Paulist Press, 1985.

Christensen, Damascene. *Not of This World: The Life and Teaching of Fr. Seraphim Rose.* Forestville, CA: Fr. Seraphim Rose Foundation, 1993.[†]

Climacus, St. John. *The Ladder of Divine Ascent.* Tr. by Colm Luibheid and Norman Russell. In *The Classics of Western Spirituality.* New York: Paulist Press, 1982.

Dostoevsky, Fyodor. *The Brothers Karamazov*. Tr. by Richard Pevear and Larissa Volokhonsky. New York: Vintage Classics, 1991.

Ephrem the Syrian, St. *Hymns.* Tr. by Kathleen E. McVey. In *The Classics of Western Spirituality.* New York: Paulist Press, 1989.

[†] I have placed *Not of this World* in the Advanced section, not because the book is particularly difficult, but because of the political nature of many of the chapters. This is a massive biography of a truly remarkable man, one who may eventually be canonized as a Saint. However, much of the book has less to do with the life of Fr. Seraphim than it does with political "adventures" of the St. Herman of Alaska Brotherhood after his death. I highly recommend this book, but the reader should be aware of the politics behind it.

RECOMMENDED READING

Evdokimov, Paul. *The Sacrament of Love: The Nuptial Mystery in the Light of the Orthodox Tradition.* Tr. by Anthony Gythiel and Victoria Steadman. Crestwood, NY: St. Vladimir's Seminary Press, 1985.

Lossky, Vladimir. *The Mystical Theology of the Orthodox Church.* Crestwood, NY: St. Vladimir's Seminary Press, 1976.

Maximus the Confessor, St. *Selected Writings.* Tr. by George C. Berthold. In *The Classics of Western Spirituality.* New York: Paulist Press, 1985.

Meyendorff, John. *Christ in Eastern Christian Thought.* Crestwood, NY: St. Vladimir's Seminary Press, 1975.

Nikodimos of the Holy Mountain, St. and St. Makarios of Corinth. *The Philokalia: The Complete Text.* 4 Vols. Tr. by Palmer, Sherrard, and Ware. London: Faber and Faber, 1979-.

Palamas, St. Gregory. *The One Hundred and Fifty Chapters.* Tr. by Robert E. Sinkewicz. Toronto: PIMS, 1988.

Rose, Eugene (Seraphim). *Nihilism: The Root of the Revolution of the Modern Age.* Forestville, CA: Fr. Seraphim Rose Foundation, 1994.

Schmemann, Alexander. *For the Life of the World: Sacraments and Orthodoxy.* Crestwood, NY: St. Vladimir's Seminary Press, 1988.

Vasileios, Archmandrite. *Hymn of Entry: Liturgy and Life in the Orthodox Church.* Tr. by Elizabeth Briere.

RECOMMENDED READING

Crestwood, NY: St. Vladimir's Seminary Press, 1984.

Vlachos, Hierotheos. *A Night in the Desert of the Holy Mountain: Discussion with a Hermit on the Jesus Prayer.* **Tr. by Effie Mavromichali. Levadia, Greece: Birth of the Theotokos Monastery, 1991.**

Yannaras, Christos. *The Freedom of Morality.* Tr. by Elizabeth Briere. Crestwood, NY: St. Vladimir's Seminary Press, 1984.

Zizioulas, John. *Being as Communion: Studies in Personhood and the Church.* Crestwood, NY: St. Vladimir's Seminary Press, 1985.

BUY 5 OR MORE ITEMS GET A 40% DISCOUNT
YES! YOU CAN MIX AND MATCH ANY ITEMS!

BOOKS
TWO PATHS Michael Whelton $22.95 (With 4 items) $13.77
Papal Monarchy Versus Collegial Tradition. Catholic or Orthodox, what is the true church?
THE SCANDAL OF GENDER Patrick Mitchell $22.95 (With 4 items) $13.77
The teachings of the Fathers on the role of women and men in the Church.
ETERNAL DAY Seth Farber $22.95 (With 4 items) $13.77
The Orthodox alternative to modern psychology
THE WAY Clark Carlton $22.95 (With 4 items) $13.77
What every Protestant should know about the Orthodox Church.
THE FAITH Clark Carlton $22.95 (With 4 items) $13.77
The best Orthodox catechism and study guide available. Endorsed by all Orthodox jurisdictions.
LETTERS TO FR. A Frank Schaeffer $22.95 (With 4 items) $13.77
How to be Orthodox in modern America.
DANCING ALONE Frank Schaeffer $20. (With 4 items) $12.00
The best selling story of personal journey of conversion.
SAVING GRANDMA Frank Schaeffer $14.95 (With 4 items) $8.97
The funniest novel ever written about growing up Protestant
PORTOFINO Frank Schaeffer $7.95 (With 4 items) $4.77
The best seller about being young, in love and a pastors child.

MUSIC CD
FIRST FRUIT CD $22.95 (With 4 items) $13.77
A fantastic CD of Byzantine chant in English.

VIDEO TAPES *Frank Schaeffer*
ORTHODOX EVANGELISM 2VHS TAPES $29.95 (With 4 items) $17.95
A great Video on how to spread the word about the Orthodox Church.
DEFENSE OF ORTHODOXY 3 VHS TAPES $59.85 (With 4 items) $35.91
The most widely used video series on Orthodoxy ever made.
TRUE STATE OF THE UNION 1 VHS TAPE $19.95 (With 4 items) $12.
The moral state of America from an Orthodox point of view. Abortion, the family other social issues.
JOURNEY TO ORTHODOXY 1 VHS TAPE $19.95 (With 4 items) $12.
How Frank Schaeffer converted to the Orthodox church. A personal journey.

CD ROM
MOUNT ATHOS CD ROM $45. (With 4 items) $27
The finest multi-media presentation of Orthodox monasticism.

FOR FASTEST SERVICE CALL TOLL FREE
800 636 2470 NON-USA CALL 978 462 7645 FAX 978 462 5079
Order over the Web! www.reginaorthodoxpress.com

Regina Orthodox Press

40% OFF For Any 5 Items or More!

Check or Credit Card **MUST** Be Enclosed

CREDIT CARD, CHECK, WEB, MAIL, CALL OR FAX YOUR ORDER TODAY!

BOOKS

# Copies_____	TWO PATHS	$22.95
# Copies_____	THE SCANDAL OF GENDER	$22.95
# Copies_____	ETERNAL DAY	$22.95
# Copies_____	THE FAITH	$22.95
# Copies_____	THE WAY	$22.95
# Copies_____	LETTERS TO Fr. ARISTOTLE	$22.95
# Copies_____	DANCING ALONE	$20.00
# Copies_____	PORTOFINO	$7.95
# Copies_____	SAVING GRANDM	$14.95

VIDEO TAPES

# Copies_____	DEFENSE OF ORTHODOXY	$59.95
# Copies_____	PERSONAL JOURNEY	$19.95
# Copies_____	ORTHODOX EVANGELISM	$29.95
# Copies_____	TRUE STATE OF THE UNION	$19.95

MUSIC CD

| # Copies_____ | FIRST FRUITS CD | 22.95 |

CD ROM

| # Copies_____ | MOUNT ATHOS CD ROM | $45.00 |

Subtotal $_____

40% DISCOUNT (ANY 5 ITEMS or MORE) $_____
Add 10% of total for shipping & handling $_____
(Non U. S. add 20% shipping & handling!)
MA residents add 5% sales tax $_____
GRAND TOTAL $_____

NAME _____
ADDRESS _____
CITY _____
STATE _____ ZIP _____
E-mail # _____
Telephone _____
MASTERCARD or VISA # _____ Exp. Date _____
SIGNATURE _____

FOR FASTEST SERVICE CALL TOLL FREE !

800 636 2470 Non US 978 462 7645 FAX 978 462 5079

Regina Orthodox Press PO Box 5288 Salisbury MA 01952

Order over the WEB! ww.**reginaorthodoxpress.com**